Plays: 3

Clap Hands Here Comes Charlie, Heaven's Blessings, Revolutionary Witness

One of Britain's most controversial dramatists, Peter Barnes has repeatedly challenged the parameters of theatrical convention. His plays have been distinguished by their biting social satire and anarchic mix of comedy and tragedy. This volume comprises his two most recent plays, *Clap Hands Here Comes Charlie* and *Heaven's Blessings*, together with *Revolutionary Witness*, commissioned and televised by the BBC in 1989.

Peter Barnes is a writer and director whose work includes *The Ruling Class* (Nottingham and Piccadilly Theatre, London, 1968), *Leonardo's Last Supper* and *Noonday Demons* (Open Space Theatre, London, 1969), *The Bewitched* (RSC, Aldwych Theatre, London, 1974), *Laughter!* (Royal Court Theatre, 1978), *Red Noses* (RSC, Barbican, 1985), *Sunsets and Glories* (West Yorkshire Playhouse, Leeds, 1990). He has won the Evening Standard Award and the John Whiting Award, 1969; Sony Best Play Award, 1981; Laurence Olivier Award, 1985; Royal Television Society Award for Best TV Play, 1987; and was nominated for an Oscar in 1993.

by the same author

Peter Barnes Plays: 1
(The Ruling Class, Leonardo's Last Supper *and* Noonday
Demons, The Bewitched, Laughter!, Barnes' People: Eight
Monologues)

Peter Barnes Plays: 2
(Red Noses, The Spirit of Man, Nobody Here but Us Chickens,
Sunsets and Glories, Bye Bye Columbus)

PETER BARNES

Plays: 3

Clap Hands Here Comes Charlie
Heaven's Blessings
Revolutionary Witness

introduced by the author

Methuen Drama

METHUEN CONTEMPORARY DRAMATISTS

This collection first published in 1996 by Methuen Drama
an imprint of Reed International Books Ltd
Michelin House, 81 Fulham Road, London SW3 6RB
and Auckland, Melbourne, Singapore and Toronto
and distributed in the United States of America
by Heinemann, a division of Reed Elsevier Inc.
361 Hanover Street, Portsmouth, New Hampshire NH 03801 3959

Front cover painting: by Peter Barnes

A CIP catalogue record for this book is available from the British Library

ISBN 0–413–69980–3

Typeset by Wilmaset Ltd, Birkenhead, Wirral

Printed in Great Britain by Cox & Wyman Ltd, Reading, Berkshire

Contents

Chronology

1965   *Sclerosis*, Aldwych Theatre, London

1968   *The Ruling Class*, Nottingham Playhouse and Piccadilly Theatre, London

1969   *Leonardo's Last Supper*, Open Space, London

1969   *Noonday Demons*, Open Space, London

1970   *Lulu*, Nottingham Playhouse, Royal Court Theatre and Apollo Theatre, London, adaptation of *Earth Spirit* and *Pandora's Box* by Frank Wedekind

1974   *The Bewitched*, Royal Shakespeare Company at the Aldwych Theatre, London

1978   *Laughter!*, Royal Court Theatre, London

1985   *Red Noses*, Royal Shakespeare Company at the Barbican Theatre, London

1990   *Sunsets and Glories*, West Yorkshire Playhouse, Leeds

1995   *Luna Park Eclipses*, Royal National Theatre Studio, London

1996   *Corpsing*, Tristan Bates Theatre, London

To Christie

Introduction

I wrote the original version of *Clap Hands Here Comes Charlie* in 1966 but it was never put on. After the production of *The Ruling Class* in 1968 I did not wish to go back to an earlier piece so I withdrew it.

However there were a few enthusiasts who knew about the play and it gained a certain underground reputation. My friend, Keith Hack, nagged me incessantly and in 1991 I gave in and rewrote it.

In the first version Charlie kills Anna at the end of Act One. Act Two is his trial, conviction and execution.

In the second version the trial and conviction of Charlie is packed into Act One which is virtually the whole of the first version. Act Two is totally new.

Act One of *Clap Hands* takes place in the 1960s and was written in the 1960s. Act Two takes place thirty years later, in the 1990s and was written in the 1990s, thirty years later.

Between Act One and Act Two, Charlie is locked up in a lunatic asylum for thirty years and then is let out into the world. Sometimes I feel I have been in an asylum with him, only there is no outside world and I haven't been released.

They say the past cannot be conquered and shouldn't be judged except by those who are willing to enter it. I did not have to enter it when I was writing *Clap Hands Here Comes Charlie*, I was already there.

Like so many others, I wake up mornings asking myself what have I been doing for the past thirty years?

There are so many kinds of fame for a writer, it's odd how many of us never know even one kind. I suspect the first requirement for contemporary fame is a total lack of humour or self-knowledge. Look how many directors ('when you have less time and can't stay, come round and see me') achieve it instantly.

I suppose success is a knack – like basket-weaving. I've never woven a half-decent one, my fingers are too clumsy. I've no sense of self, artificial or natural and I've spent too long killing geese that lay those golden eggs. Be that as it may and I doubt if it ever was, I can have no complaints. I picked the field to plough and the furrows are still straight.

Thirty years ago I said I wrote to change the world but, of course, I haven't changed anything. The sun doesn't rise in the West, the rivers don't run backwards, the seas never stand still or the rain fall upwards and I still use both hands to brush my teeth. Worse, the strong still get more and the weak ones fade. They keep the million-orbed light from us which beams down as on the first day of creation.

For thirty years I've been trying to light the storm with mirrors, whirlpools, balloons, moonglow, starbursts. In that time I have discovered a little about writing, like the difference between signature and style. Signature is the audible voice, the visible colour. Style is the thread, the hoop that holds focus. But signature can turn into style, truth caught with artistry in a strong net of words. In those thirty years I've also found out I always meant what I didn't say, which is bitter. There's no clear path, no path at all.

I haven't abandoned my principles but I realise I've been lucky, I've never been forced to. For example, I have not been persecuted by the police because my wife's hair looked wild and I had a beard when our passport photographs were taken. So I hope I've remained true to that multi-tongued 'vision thing' they talk about.

In thirty years a parrot which barked like a dog and said 'quack, quack' was stolen from a house in Maidenhead, a scientist at a fish farm in South Uist spent two days in hospital after a salmon slapped him in the face with its tail and my mother and so many others have been washed away to sea.

I used to think I couldn't exist without the oxygen of laughter but I realise I need it less and less.

'I'm sorry, m'lud, but I'm unable to continue without an injection of nerve gas.'
'Hello, out there, can you tell me the way to optimism?'

Peter Barnes
1996

Clap Hands
Here Comes Charlie

Characters

Gunboat Smith
Zacchaeus
Joe Gaff
Warden
Michael Aylmer
Diana Bishop
Charles Ketchum
Technician
Joan Aylmer
Judge
Ms Trevor
Clerk of the Court
Detective Inspector Poole
Gerald Woods
John Euston
Norman Stoner
Dr Nathaniel Burgess
Peter Barnes
Inspector's Voice
Arthur Sidley
Mrs Aylmer
Nurse Dudley
Dr Ford
Death
Nicolaus
Angels, Waiters, Derelicts

Act One

Scene One

A street band plays 'Clap Hands, Here Comes Charlie'.

Lights up. Interior Mission Lodging House, Autumn 1964. A bare room with eight beds, four either side. A notice on the door Upstage Centre reads: 'Jesus Saves'.

Three members of the street band, **Gunboat Smith, Joe Gaff** *and* **Zacchaeus** *are just getting up whilst the fourth is asleep on his bed Downstage Left.*

Smith *is dressed in an army greatcoat two sizes too small and with bulging pockets. He sits on the edge of his bed laboriously pulling on old boots.*

Smith Poo' pee . . . eeeee . . . 'es o' para' . . . sick parade . . . What 'appens t'all t'all, t'all, the women? . . . an' the pox doctor? . . . what 'appens t'all the women who 'aven't been raped, what 'appens? . . .

Coughing violently **Zacchaeus** *crosses to his torn raincoat on a chair and pulls out a bottle.*

Zacchaeus Plain jake's der stuff fer breakfast. Jus' plain jake, plain jake. Dirty sheets, cigarette burns, out.

Joe Gaff *has unwrapped a packet of thick bread sandwiches and spreads the wrapping paper on the bed as a tablecloth, takes a knife, fork, cruet-set and dirty serviette from his pockets, and lays them out.*

Gaff Arrrh . . . Arrrh . . . Arrrh . . . (*Pulls out an old copy of* The Times *from under his vest.*) Arrrh? . . . Arrrh? . . . Arrrh? (*He puts on his battered bowler hat.*) Ahhhhh! (*He starts eating.*)

Smith (*slowly, rolling a cigarette*) I done nothin' . . . whaa . . . no difference . . . schools, prisons, police stations . . . Aggie knows . . . What y'doing with that rubbish? . . . It's all turban tit-tarting . . .

He lights the cigarette and it goes up in flames. Unperturbed, he immediately starts rolling another.

They can't touch me . . . what abat the bullets and the girls w-w-waving goodbye? . . .

Zacchaeus *has unwrapped two spoons from a cloth which he rubs.*

Zacchaeus No place for sitting down, lying down. Oh Jaysus, oh Jaysus, they let pygmies run wild on Hampstead Heath, eighteen months hard and fifteen of the best.

Gaff I'm wired. My back teeth are wired. They send me messages from beyond and further. Tap-tap-tap . . . That's how I get advanced warning about the Lituanians and others of the same ilk. Warnings won't stop 'em but at least I'm prepared.

Zacchaeus Me brother put de Valera in power, and we've never heard from him since.

Smith In them days . . . pinch whoring an' all . . . we didn't stand a chance . . . Gi' us some plain jake, Zac . . . (*Takes a rubber plunger from his pocket.*) Gi' us . . .

Gaff (*rubbing his chest*) Wired AC/DC. Fed straight into my nerve ends. I can hear it all plain as a pikestaff but nobody else can. Top secret. Mum's the word.

Zacchaeus *tests his spoons by hitting them together on his elbow and knee.*

Zacchaeus Jaysus, Jaysus. God's on his knees nailed to the Cross.

Smith Gi' us some jake.

Zacchaeus No, you's a Conshie!

As **Smith** *jabs at* **Zacchaeus** *with his plunger, the* **Warden** *enters Upstage Centre with* **Michael Aylmer** *and* **Diana Bishop**.

Warden You see, Mr Aylmer, only four beds occupied. In the old days we packed 'em in, twelve a room. Times change. Now they prefer to skipper out – Victoria Station and the more fashionable bombsites . . . Now, pay attention, men. This is Mr Michael Aylmer. And this is his secretary, Miss Bishop.

No response from the others. They are too busy leaving. **Gaff** *quickly clears away his breakfast, stuffing the newspaper back up his vest, whilst* **Zacchaeus** *puts on his raincoat and* **Smith** *lumbers back to his bed.*

Aylmer There's nothing to be afraid of, gentlemen. I'm in television.

Gaff Mea culpa, mea culpa.

Aylmer We want to do a programme.

Smith Why's that then?

Aylmer Why's what?

Smith You got nothing on me.

Aylmer We don't want to get anything on you. The programme's about men and women like yourself, outside society.

Diana We've already done gipsies, schizophrenics and drug addicts.

Zacchaeus Drink's me curse, miss. Drink. Plain jake. I don't grow Indian hemp in da flower beds like some. Oh Jaysus, I'm down, I'm down, but I haven't gone ta pot.

Gaff Doctors are the worst drug addicts. And Lituanians of course. But they're into everything.

Aylmer This programme's about buskers, street entertainers. That's why I want you gentlemen to help. There's ten pounds each in it for you.

About to leave, they all stop and look at him.

Zacchaeus Is dat right, sir, not pennies, not pennies? What good is pennies for people like us?

Smith Pennies is no good.

Aylmer Pounds, not pennies. Just for talking. That's not so hard, is it?

They all nod eagerly.

Warden You see, when there's money involved, they'll listen. Some of 'em have more hidden away than you or me.

Aylmer *gestures discreetly to* **Diana**, *who takes the* **Warden**'s *arm and guides him firmly Upstage.*

Aylmer Gentlemen, I want to get to know you a little before we actually do the programme.

Smith Gi' us a fag, sir.

Aylmer *hands him a packet of cigarettes.* **Smith** *takes three, and by the time the others have helped themselves, it is empty.*

Aylmer You're Mr . . . ?

Gaff Joseph Gaff, now I'm busted. But it'll be Joseph Gaff *Esquire* again once I'm back on my feet.

Aylmer How long've you been playing together, Joseph?

Gaff Two weeks. Pro tem. We never stay together. Two's company, three's a crowd.

Zacchaeus (*hitting himself on elbow and head with his spoons*) They'll always want Zacchaeus while he can click the silvers.

Aylmer Zacchaeus? That's an extraordinary name.

Zacchaeus Zacchaeus by name and Zacchaeus by nature, sir.

Smith (*saluting*)   Gunboat Smith, sir, Number 2487640, first class.

Aylmer   Why're you called Gunboat?

Smith   'Cause I got big feet.

Zacchaeus   Send a gunboat up the Thames!

Aylmer *notices the fourth man, still asleep on the bed.*

Aylmer   Someone we missed. Is he part of the band?

Gaff   It depends on this and that. He only joined a couple of days ago.

Smith   'E just come.

Zacchaeus   Like da Holy Ghost.

Aylmer   We'd better wake him up then.

Gaff   He's all right to tell stories about but it's different him in the flesh.

Zacchaeus   Yous don't want him in the flesh if yous can help it.

Smith   Jankers for life.

Warden   Let sleeping dogs lie, Mr Aylmer.

Aylmer   Where would the world be if dogs were left to lie? They're man's best friend.

Warden   Not this one.

They are all gathered round the bed looking down at the sleeping man.

Zacchaeus   Dat's One-Eyed Charlie Ketchum.

Smith   'E's not like us.

Gaff   I'm pretty certain he's a Lituanian.

There are long drawn-out intakes of breath as **Aylmer** *shakes the sleeping* **Ketchum**.

Aylmer   Charlie, Charlie. Come on, Charlie. (*The man rolls over.*) Sorry I had to wake you.

Ketchum   Piss off!

Aylmer   I want to talk to you.

Ketchum   Piss off, 'afore I do it on you!

Aylmer *continues shaking him. With a growl* **Ketchum** *finally rouses himself. He has thick matted hair and a black eye-patch over his left eye. He could be any age.*

Aylmer   Charlie, we're doing a television programme and we didn't want to leave you out.

Ketchum   A man can't even get a decent kip-down nowadays. I was just dreaming it up – well you get a better class of woman that way – there I was in Heaven eating cheese an' onion flavoured crisps and then you comes on shouting 'Charlie, Charlie' . . . Now I'm blocked. You'll be sorry . . . (*He sees* **Diana** *for the first time.*) Oh. Oh. Oh. (*He scrambles up in front of her on the bed.*) Charlie de Witt Ketchum at yer service . . . (*She winces.*) It's the Ketchum stink, kills flies at twenty feet, flowers at thirty, it's better than all yer DDT's and such.

As she moves away a **TV Technician** *enters Upstage Centre and signals to* **Aylmer**.

Aylmer   Looks like our equipment's arrived. I wonder if you'd all mind giving us a hand?

Smith   Sir!

Warden   Hop to it, men.

As they help the **Technician** *move the bed more Upstage,* **Aylmer** *remains with* **Ketchum**, *who is still staring after* **Diana**.

Ketchum   Prime slice of brisket, but that's no bloody excuse fer what you did. You saw the notice on the door 'DO NOT DISTURB'. I'll have no truck wi', no truck wi'.

Aylmer   I take it you don't want to be in the show?

Ketchum Yer taking nothing of what's mine, mister. The show's no good without Charlie.

The **Technician** *calls* **Aylmer** *over.* **Ketchum** *stumbles off the bed and spitting on a large rag, he wipes his face, unbuttons his jacket and rubs his bare chest. Next, he ties a thick scarf round his neck like a cravat and passes a comb with only two teeth over his matted hair and looks at himself admiringly in a broken hand-mirror.*

Ketchum Oh lovely, lovely Charlie.

Pulling a string bag from under the bed, he takes out a row of medals strung on a cord and pins them on his jacket. Throwing out his chest, he tries to attract **Diana**'s *attention by pointing to the medals.*

Ketchum Gave 'em a taste of British steel. *Yah!*

Diana *pays no attention as the* **Technician** *enters with arc lights and cables.* **Smith, Zacchaeus** *and* **Gaff** *drift Downstage Right.* **Ketchum** *shambles over to them, waving his trumpet.*

Ketchum This lot couldn't organise a piss-up in a brewery, we'll show 'em what British boys are made of.

Gaff I know what's right. I've done cost accounting before I was busted: profit and loss, double entry, fixed assets. D-e-p-r-e-c-i-a-t-i-o-n-s. The contract states one performance. Net.

Ketchum It's just practice. Everybody needs practice – Alastair McWhilkie the man with the fourteen-foot beard, Eko and Iko the two Albino Negroes, Dainty Irene the woman with the cast-iron jaw, the Cherry Sisters, 'Broomstick' Elliott, Captain Sorcho and his Monster Submarine Show – they all needed practice.

Zacchaeus Even da best Irish silvers need practice.

Gaff No harm in practice, I suppose. Practice is different from playing for real.

Zacchaeus *takes out his spoons.* **Smith** *and* **Gaff** *get their instruments.*

Ketchum   Quick-quick-quick, we'll miss the tide.

They line up with their hands on the shoulder of the man in front. **Ketchum** *stamps his foot three times.* **Aylmer** *and the others look round in surprise.*

Ketchum (*singing*)   'Rolling round the world, looking for the sunshine, that never seems to come our way . . . Rolling round the world, where every little milestone, seems to look at us and say . . .'

The **Technician** *throws up his papers in fright as* **Ketchum** *gives a blast on his trumpet and, with spoons clicking, banjo and sax playing,* **Ketchum** *leads the band raggedly Upstage.* **Aylmer** *doubles up with laughter as the band, still attempting to play, stumble into the equipment. At the height of the noise and confusion there is a loud scream. All turn to* **Diana** *and* **Ketchum** *who have become entangled.*

Diana   You filthy, disgusting pig!

There is a ripping sound as she breaks free and runs out. All eyes now turn to **Ketchum**.

Ketchum   Knickers! They came away in my hand. Just blown together. (*He holds up a pair of torn panties.*) Damn British workmanship. Right, lads, once more with feeling.

They resume playing loudly.

Blackout.

Scene Two

Lights up on **Aylmer**'s *living-room.*

A window Upstage Centre overlooks a balcony. Stage Left packed bookshelves, radiogram and a bust of Bertrand

*Russell. Door Upstage Right to the corridor and flat
entrance. Sofa, Downstage Right.*

Joan Aylmer *stands by the television set as* **Aylmer** *enters
Stage Right, slightly drunk. She crosses and kisses him.*

Joan   Your programme was very good, Michael. I'll get
you something to eat. It's obvious you don't need
anything to drink. Where on earth did you dig up that
character with the trumpet?

Aylmer   You liked him, then?

Joan   Fabulous.

Aylmer   That's good. Charlie!

Ketchum *appears in the doorway Upstage Right carrying
his string-bag.*

Aylmer   Meet One-Eyed Charlie Ketchum.

Ketchum   The virgin's friend. Where's the boghouse?

Joan   The what?

Ketchum   Bog-house, krapper, loo, thunder-box.

Aylmer   Second door on the left. You don't have to take
your trumpet.

Ketchum   Sometimes I just like to sit an' blow both
ends against the middle.

He exits.

Joan   The answer's 'no', Michael. He can't stay here.

Aylmer   Just for the weekend. Two days. It's partly my
fault he got thrown out of his hostel, so I asked him here.
It's not entirely altruistic. I've decided to do a special
programme on him.

Joan   Why?

Aylmer   You said yourself he's fabulous. He's what I've
been looking for, the real thing, one hundred per cent
proof.

Joan   Remember when you brought home those Golders Green gipsies to spend Christmas with us. I suppose I'll have to get rid of Mr Ketchum the same way. Fortunately they all prefer hard cash to soft living.

Aylmer   Not Ketchum.

Joan   Give him the choice – money or spending the weekend here with us!

Aylmer (*giving her some notes*)   You don't understand, Charlie's the last of the Swagmen, the Moon-Men, the Sons of Rest. He's the last Free Spirit.

Ketchum *lurches back, holding up his trousers.*

Ketchum   I want . . .

Joan   I know what you want, Mr Ketchum. (*Gives him the money.*) Here, that should be enough for you.

Ketchum   You use this do you? I'm out of touch, on the road. But I'm impressed and it takes a lot to impress yours truly, who's been everywhere, seen everything. Better have a few more, Missus.

Joan   You see, he wants a few more. There's no more, Mr Ketchum.

Ketchum   But I've got a huge tender bott.

Aylmer   What are you talking about?

Ketchum   Lavo-paper. (*Mimes wiping his behind.*) No paper in the bog. (*Crumples notes.*) There ain't enough 'ere to cover a flea's backside.

Joan   You can't wipe yourself with pound notes!

Ketchum   I always knew the rich papered the wall with the stuff, but using it as lavo-paper, that's something the Bolshies'll latch onto . . . (*Feels the notes.*) On second thoughts, they're terrible hard, feel the edges. No mercy 'ere for a tender bott like mine.

Joan *snatches the money back and gives him a magazine lying handy.*

Joan   Here, try this on your tender bott.

Aylmer   Joan, that's the *New Statesman*!

Ketchum (*moving off, stroking the magazine*)   Yus, yus
. . . soft . . . soft . . . bummy soft . . . soft . . . soft . . .

Ketchum *exits Stage Right.*

Aylmer   You should've given him *The Times*.

Joan   Michael, he's dangerous! He's not our problem.

Aylmer   He's not a problem, he's a phenomenon.
That's why I want to get him on tape. But there *is* a risk
and I shouldn't've asked you to share it. Except we've
always shared everything. But you're right.

Joan   You mean you're sure I'm wrong.

Aylmer   I'll tell him to go. It was a mad idea.

Joan   I don't object to a little madness, within reason. I
suppose we can survive two days.

They kiss.

But there's one condition. He'll have to wash.

Ketchum *re-enters, Stage Right.*

Ketchum   Wash?! So that's yer filthy game. I'm
shoving off!

Joan   Goodbye, Charlie.

Aylmer   Don't you want to eat?

Ketchum   Always ready fer a gut-bash but I got me
pride and things.

Aylmer   What do you want? Anything you like?

Ketchum   Like . . . ? Well, there's sardines, I like
sardines. I's eaten 'undreds o' the slippery little bastards
in me time. (*Mimes tossing a sardine into his mouth.*) Honk-
honk. (*He claps his hands like a seal.*) Sardines 'ave a
special sardiney taste. Mulligatawny soup? You got any
mulligatawny soup, herrings in oatmeal, nettle beer and

trotter stew? You don't see no fatty trotter stew nowadays, an' cow-heel brawn, that's something else again. (*He ties a filthy rag round his neck like a bib.*) Bosworth jumbles and forcemeat balls! It's snouts in the trough, lads, for over-bottom cake, hedgerow jam and mushroom pickle. Oysters! Forty dozen of the best, me good man. Gi' me nob's grub every time, kidneys in champagne, anchovy cheese and a bloody great boar's head with titchy paper 'orns, glass eyeballs and a orange stuck in its cake-'ole and then there's jellies firm as young girls' tits bouncing an' shaking, what stuff, what stuff . . .

Lights dim to a spot on him.

Ever had badger pie or larks baked in goose-liver? Marigold eggs? Ever had marigold eggs, Jerusalem artichokes, Queen of Sheba cake, angels on horseback, star-gazey pie, grains of paradise? . . . *Ahhh . . . Ahhh . . .*

Spot out on his drooling cries.

Scene Three

Spot up immediately on a bath Downstage Centre.
Ketchum *appears, clad only in filthy underwear and torn newspapers. Seeing the audience he covers his crotch with his hands.* **Aylmer** *enters Stage Right with soap and a large towel embroidered with 'His', and* **Joan** *enters Stage Left with a scrubbing brush and a towel embroidered with 'Hers'.*

Ketchum   No, I won't wash! Dirty is protection against the cold. What 'appens to all those hoppy little fellas I give bread and board to if I wash? They'll be drowned if I wash, I'll lose me stink if I wash and I'll starve if I lose me stink, 'cause all I 'ave to do is sidle up to an easy mark, downwind, stick out me hand and he'll pay just to get out of smelling distance. But one wash and it's all over. One wash and I'm left clean and stoney back on the Holyhead Road. I'll be sat there smelling of carbolic, all me strength washed away. Missus, missus, I've seen men go bald overnight with too much washing. I won't wash!

Aylmer   You have to if you want to see the beautiful Miss Bishop again, Charlie. So off with that stinking underwear!

Ketchum   You mean, get in *naked*! You bloody perverts!

Joan   If you're that modest we'll do it in the dark.

She switches off the light as they make a grab for him. Cries of terror from the darkness, then a tremendous shout and a great splash. Silence.

Joan's voice   There, everything all right now?

Ketchum's voice   No, it ain't! Where's me bleeding rubber duck?

Scene Four

Spot up immediately on a hairy leg and thigh poked provocatively out of Wings Right. **Ketchum** *emerges in a silk dressing-gown and slippers.*

Ketchum (*singing*)   'I'm Bert. / Perhaps you've 'eard of me, Bert. / You've had word of me / Jogging along, hearty and strong, living on plates of fresh air. / I dress up in fashion and when I'm feeling depressed / Shave from my snuff / All the whiskers and fluff. / Stick my hat on and toddle up West. / I'm Burlington Bertie, / I rise at ten thirty / and saunter along like a Toff. / I walk down the Strand / With my gloves in my hand / Then I walk down again with 'em off. / I'm all airs and graces / Correct easy paces. / Without food so long / I've forgot where my face is. / I'm Bert, Bert / I haven't a shirt / But my people are well-off you know. / Nearly everyone knows me. / From Smith to Lord Roseberry, / I'm Burlington Bertie from Bow.'

The sound of clapping. **Ketchum** *bows. Lights up to show* **Aylmer** *sitting on the sofa applauding. There is a tape-recorder on the coffee-table in front of him.*

Ketchum   I'm just bumming me chat. All that washing's loosened the muscles of my mind. I know hundreds of the old 'uns.

Aylmer   Good, but I want to get on with our talk.

Ketchum   Yak-yak-yak.

Aylmer   You shouldn't despise talk, Charlie, particularly as you never stop yourself. To talk is to know you're alive. Hell isn't fire and ice, but dead silence.

Ketchum   I don't believe in dying.

Aylmer (*switching on recorder*)   Tell me more.

Ketchum   If they're going to know about Charlie, tell 'em he's a high-flying goer, *whoosh*. Top Cock o' the Holyhead Road, *whoosh*.

Aylmer   What's a Top Cock?

Ketchum   Top man on his road, still would be if I hadn't found that trumpet in a ditch. Always wanted to play in a proper band like Orville Strumm and his Ukelele Rascals. Dago Brown the Maltese piano-tuner's Top Cock now. You gets a lot of riff-raff on the road. That's only natural, it takes guts to be a failure.

Aylmer   How did you start on the road?

Ketchum   The War, served King and Country, hearth and home, Cain and Abel. Get yer hair cut! I still get stingin' pains in me head. Couldn't settle nine to five in Civvy Street, started knocking 'em back, blocked on Brasso and picking up fag-ends to clear the mind.

Aylmer   So that's how you started?

Ketchum   Started what?

Aylmer   On the road.

Ketchum A woman – what else? – God bless the ladies! It happened when I was getting spliced to young Lydia Braithwaite. It were a real snob wedding 'cause the bride was only three months pregnant. And that's the living truth.

Aylmer It can't be. Both those stories can't be true.

Ketchum Truth is as long as long. You're not calling me a liar in yer own home I hope?! (*Suddenly noticing the bust.*) It's Pie-Face Pearson!

Aylmer That's Bertrand Russell, the philosopher. Now I want the truth, Charlie.

Ketchum It's Pie-Face Pearson. Bloody artist, used to con the marks by telling 'em he were a true Christian. 'Brother, the Brotherhood of the Road is truly the Brotherhood of Christ.' Bloody artist, passed away in the odour of sanctity, found frozen to death in a ladies loo half-way up Dollis Hill. A mystery that. Nobody never found out what a man like Pearson was doing halfway up Dollis Hill!

Aylmer No, that's Bertrand Russell, Earl Russell. I knew him at Cambridge.

Ketchum 'You're a Christian, thank Christ, Christ wasn't', he'd always say. 'Remember Jesus saves, but Moses invests.' (*Picks up his trumpet and comes to attention.*) Farewell old Pie, at the coming up and the going down we remember . . . (*He plays a few shaky bars of the 'Last Post'.*)

Aylmer Damn you, it's Russell!

Ketchum Don't mean no harm, sir. (*Peers at the bust.*) Yus, yus, you're right, you're right, 'tain't him, looks like him but 'tain't him, more like his brother.

Aylmer Whose brother?

Ketchum Pie-Face Pearson.

Aylmer Will you shut up about Pie-Face Pearson!

Joan *enters Stage Right carrying a pile of men's clothes and dumps them on a chair.*

Joan   Some of your things, Michael. I thought Mr Ketchum could use them.

Ketchum   What you done to me ol' togs?

Joan   Nothing. They crawled to the incinerator without any help from me.

Ketchum   You's burnt me best Sunday clobber?! That's hand-picked stuff! You realise I've been voted the best-dressed dosser on the Holyhead Road every year since 1950? Them boots of mine was thrown at me by the Earl of Arran's footman back in '47. I tell you those clothes was full of memories, we've done things, been places.

As **Diana** *enters Stage Right carrying a briefcase, he rushes over and falls on his knees in front of her.*

Ketchum   It's my turtle dove, me piece of French muslin.

Joan   What do you use, Diana, aniseed?

Ketchum (*getting up*)   You're right, I've been caught with me short and curlies showing. (*Grabs clothes.*) I got presents for you, don't move now, then or later.

He rushes out Stage Right with the clothes.

Aylmer   I'm sorry, Diana, it's not part of your job to cope with the Charlie Ketchums of this world.

Joan   Though it does seem to be mine.

Diana   Don't worry. I can deal with him, Michael. I've confirmed you'll be at Broadcasting House at two thirty . . . Your talk.

Aylmer   I'd forgotten. I can't leave you alone with him, Joan.

Joan   I told you it'd be impossible having him here.

Aylmer If we can't get someone over to stay with you, I'll cancel the talk.

Joan Don't be ridiculous. He's obnoxious but harmless.

Ketchum *dances in Upstage Left scattering sand on the floor. He wears trousers which only reach to his shins, and a long sweater which falls over his behind. He tears at a tightly rolled newspaper, stuffing the pieces into his pocket, as he dances on the sand.*

Ketchum (*singing*) 'Bye-bye rainy days, bye-bye snow. / Got no use for you, got to go. / Rolling round the world. / Looking for the sunshine / I know I'm going to find one day . . .'

He finishes by skidding up to an astonished **Diana** *and presenting her with a four-foot-high fir tree he has made out of the torn paper.*

Lights out.

Scene Five

Aylmer's voice The difference between tragedy and comedy is that comedy offers no hope. Tragedy shows man broken by an incomprehensible fate, it presumes man is worth breaking. Comedy offers no such sops to pride . . .

As it is clicked off, lights up on **Aylmer**'s *living-room.* **Joan** *has just switched off the radio.* **Ketchum** *is slouched impatiently against the bookshelf.*

Joan They have it on tape. I can hear it later.

Ketchum Yak-yak-yak.

Joan Have you always got to be the centre of attention, Ketchum?

Ketchum Who else is there? Let's have a noggin after all that yakking. (*He crosses to the cocktail cabinet.*) A

Ketchum special fer à la carte people. (*He pulls out the cork of the bottle with his teeth and slops whisky into glasses.*) Of course it should be spiked with meths, to give it zzzz-zing. Every house should have meths fer cooking purposes. Meths gives roast beef that extra homely touch.

He hands the drink to **Joan**.

Joan   I'll try to remember to keep a bottle in stock. You're a heavy drinker?

Ketchum   Dresses up, knickers down! (*Drinks.*) If it's wet I'll drink it while the mood's on me and it's cold outside and the little men in hobnail boots start thumping and farting abat in my mind. Then it's gin, beer, red biddy or 'Charlie's Number One' – that's coal gas pumped through ginger beer, real thirst-quench specially with a slice of lemon floating on the top. The trick is to open yer mouth wide when yer guzzling the stuff to keep it from touching yer teeth and dissolving the enamel – sent Josser Tobins blind as a bat.

Joan   Is that how you lost your eye?

Ketchum   No. Maude Chambers. All teeth and tits was Maude, she must've known I was after an eyeful at the keyhole 'cause a bloody eyeful is what she gave me. *Arrr*, blinded by love. Now it's got me again.

Joan   Miss Bishop might not want you, Charlie – ever thought of that?

Ketchum   Not want Charlie, that's a good one, missus.

Joan   She might be in love with somebody else.

Ketchum   Your hubby like. S'natural, old Flannel-Mouth's just a stand-in till her prince came a-riding by.

Joan   So, you think Diana's attracted to Michael? I think so too. As you say, it's natural. If I wasn't in love with him I'd be attracted too. Michael's special. I'm lucky he's a one-woman man.

Ketchum A one-woman man. Horrible. 'Tain't natural.

Joan You've known lots of women, Charlie?

Ketchum See these teeth? I wore 'em out making love. I came out of a woman and I'm always trying to get back inside.

Joan What's the secret of your fatal attraction?

Ketchum My mind – that's what gets 'em. A mind like mine could turn the world upside-down in a week. I'm on the Inner Council of Gipsies I know so much. I know that bumble bees have two stomachs, eyebrows are there to keep the sweat from falling into yer eyeballs, and Santa Claus is God on National Assistance. See, see, I'm full of fact and fancy, that's what the skirts like.

Joan (*laughing*) Where did you learn this marvellous technique, Charlie?

Ketchum (*singing*) 'I'm following in father's footsteps, / I'm following the dear old dad. / He's just in front with a fine big girl / So I thought I'd have one as well. / Now I don't know where I'm going, / But when I get there I'll be glad. / Oh, I'm following in father's footsteps, / Yes, I'm following the dear old dad.' (*He pulls* **Joan** *off the sofa.*) All together now . . .

Ketchum } (*singing and dancing*) 'We don't know
Joan   } where we're going, / But when we get there we'll be glad. / We're following in father's footsteps, / Yes, we're following the dear old dad.'

They finish Stage Centre, **Joan** *laughing.*

Ketchum That were good, missus.

Joan You don't have to keep calling me missus, the name's Joan.

Ketchum Joan . . . Joany . . .

Without warning he sweeps her into his arms and kisses her.
Joan *is too astounded to resist. The action is so absurd and*
Ketchum *so ridiculous that* **Joan** *throughout is half-laughing, half-raging.*

Joan   Ketchum!

Ketchum   I got the message – bip – bip – bip . . .

Joan   I'll scream . . .

She opens her mouth to scream, instead bursts into hysterical laughter.

Ketchum   You like Charlie's kisses? Everybody likes Charlie's Grade-One, super slip-slops.

Joan   I don't, you bloody great oaf!

Ketchum   Why don't you like Charlie's slip-slops?

Joan   Because your breath stinks!

Ketchum *lets go of her and* **Joan** *falls flat on the floor with a thud.* **Ketchum** *staggers to the mantelpiece, grabs the flowers in the vase and eats their heads off. Stumbling back, he breathes straight into her face.*

Ketchum   Soft heart, soft mouth and my breath smelling like all the flowers in June. Bet you didn't know ducks always lay their eggs in the morning, *plop-plop*. Once I was so broke, I didn't have a roof to me mouth . . .

Despite herself, **Joan** *can't stop giggling.* **Ketchum** *scoops her up in his arms.*

Joan   Ketchum!

Ketchum   Coochie-coochie, did you know grasshoppers can jump twenty times their own height? Coochie-coochie. Let's get the needle in the wax and hear the music.

He drops **Joan** *on the sofa and dives on top of her while trying to take off his trousers.*

Joan   Keep off! . . . You dirty great . . . Stop! . . . Ketchum . . . you hairy . . . Eeee . . . Eeee . . .

She tails off into hysterical laughter.

Lights out.

Scene Six

Spot up Downstage Centre on **Ketchum** *sitting fully clothed on a toilet enclosed on three sides by white walls, his trumpet on the floor beside him.*

Ketchum   To scarper or to stick here, that's the bleeding question. Out there it's cold. But my plates of meat are twitching. Still it's an easy mark here, three gut-bashes a day and a soft kip-down. But I got to breathe again. But what if old Flannel-Mouth finds out I've been sniffing his missus? His bones have soft centres but he might turn nasty, there's something strange abat him, look at this place for starters, who's ever seen a loo looking clean as a hospital on a Monday? I've unloaded freight in every bog-house south of the Pennines, some no more than holes in the ground, others with marble walls and silver toilet seats, but I never seen one like this. Where's the writing on the walls, where's the drawings, messages and poems? And the names: Jock, Angus, Dusty, Ron, Annie, Betty Pilchard, Walter Noab, Snead Urn, ring 273 4827. Every name you read on a bog-house wall is real, the messages too . . . 'Stamp Out Red Ants! . . . I wear women's knickers and I'm eighty-eight years old . . . Sue Wilson and Nobody Else.' And the words of wisdom you won't find in no classroom. I got me education from the bog-house walls of England. 'Love thy neighbour, but don't get caught doing it.' . . . 'Don't throw yer toothpicks in the bowl, the crabs here can pole-vault.' What riches! But here there's nothing – white tiles! You can't even scratch anything on white tiles . . . I'm moving on, *whoosh* . . . But what abat me honey-star, Diana? Can't leave her behind. Steady, Charlie, you've never had no partner on the Toby 'afore. Ah, but times are changing and she's beautiful. She can hoof the Toby with me! . . . Best place to make up yer mind, sitting on a throne, that's why kings and queens have thrones to sit on. God save the Queen! And everybody else!

He stands to attention and pulls the toilet chain.

Blackout to the sound of the toilet flushing.

Scene Seven

Lights up immediately on the living-room. **Aylmer** *is on the sofa adjusting the tape-recorder as* **Joan** *paces.*

Aylmer   What exactly did he do?

Joan   The usual – sang, danced, told jokes. He's the original all-round entertainer.

Aylmer   Sounds as if he was on top of his form.

Joan   He was on top, all right, Michael. He's a man without inhibitions and men without inhibitions are animals. He's got to go.

Aylmer   I agree. He's a wonderful monster to read about but impossible to live with.

Joan   Do you love me?

Aylmer   Always.

They kiss as **Ketchum** *enters Downstage Left in his overcoat and carrying his string bag.*

Ketchum   I'm off.

Aylmer   You're leaving?

Ketchum   Like a fart in a bottle, where's me buttered crumpet, Di?

Aylmer   She's due any minute.

Ketchum   I got hot news for her. She can come with me on the Toby!

Aylmer   She might take some persuading.

Joan Charlie's a most persuasive fellow when he puts his mind to it.

She exits into bedroom, Stage Right.

Aylmer I'm sorry you're going, Charlie. I invited some friends round to meet you.

Ketchum (*popping table-lighter into his bag*) I can't meet every Tom, Dick and Jeffrey who wants to scrap up an acquaintance.

Aylmer Put that back. What else have you taken?

Taking the string bag from him, he discovers an alarm clock, knife, scrubbing-brush, toilet-roll and stockings inside.

Ketchum Those are mine. Odds and rag-ends you gave me. Tokens of your esteem, you said.

Aylmer What else have you got hidden?

He pulls open **Ketchum**'s *overcoat to show he has* **Aylmer**'s *silk dressing-gown underneath.*

Aylmer Take it off!!

Ketchum (*ripping off coat and gown*) There's gratitude, if me throat was on fire you wouldn't spit in me mouth!

Aylmer I'll give you something, but you're not stealing.

Ketchum Stealing?! These are gifts. I wouldn't have 'em now, not never. (*Puts coat back on.*) I'll just take what's mine and go.

He picks up the bust.

Aylmer Put it back!

As **Aylmer** *yanks the bust from him,* **Joan** *comes back with a cut-glass salad bowl.*

Joan I found this under his bed.

Aylmer What were you doing with that, Charlie?

Ketchum What comes natural. You should always have a jerry-pot to hand at night. It's hygienic.

Aylmer Hygienic!? That's not a jerry-pot. It's a salad bowl. We *eat* out of it.

Ketchum Eat out of it? Never heard anything so *filthy!*

Diana *enters and* **Ketchum** *rushes to her.*

Ketchum It's me hot-nifty . . .

Joan Charlie's got something important to tell you, Diana.

Ketchum Yes, but there's too many ears a-flappin'. If you don't mind, Miss D and I have some cud to chew over.

Aylmer Miss Bishop can't be left alone with you, Charlie.

Joan But *I* could.

Diana There's no problem.

Aylmer No nonsense now, Ketchum.

Aylmer *and* **Joan** *exit to the kitchen Upstage Right.*

Ketchum Anybody'd think he owned the place.

Diana What is it?

Ketchum It's hard . . . Never had the glamour put on me 'afore. When I'm with you it's like I got a hot sun on me back, shoes on me feet and an empty road ahead. I'm a young shaver again all pimply-shy. (*Singing.*) 'I'm shy, little Diana, I'm shy. / It does seem so naughty, oh my. / Kissing is nice, I've often heard say. / But still how to do it I don't know the way. / 'Cos I'm shy . . .'

Diana Stop it! What do you want?

Ketchum Nowt, I'm giving . . . Di, you can join me hoofing the pad, just the two of us under the blue blanket, doing the starry!

Diana You're mad. You don't really expect me to go off with a filthy ignorant old tramp?!

Ketchum I should hope not, you're going with *me*!

Diana I don't even like you.

Ketchum Don't even like meself, all ponced and smelling of carbolic. But you just wait, I'll be sweet Charlie agin or my name isn't Harrison Clegg.

Diana I know the kind of man I want, and it isn't you. He must be sincere, dedicated, sensitive. I'll devote myself to him, so he'll have to earn enough money for both of us.

Ketchum Money? You ain't a money-grubber after the axle-grease, the rhino? You can't be one of those. You're like me. If I got more than a few copper coins in me pocket at the end of the day I gets windy, 'tain't natural. So long as a man's got his fill of bangers, bacey, booze and bints, what's he want with tons of rhino weighing him down? What's the good of rhino when yer gut-sack's full? . . . (*Suddenly raging at the audience.*) But you lot'd skin cow-turds if there was money in it! You'd hold yer noses with one hand and skin away like mad with the other . . . (*He mimes skinning action.*) One-two-three-ugh, one-two-three-ugh. (*To* **Diana**.) But we ain't like them. We're normal.

Diana I'm not! So you see it's hopeless, Ketchum. I must have a man with money. At least a thousand pounds to start with.

Ketchum Where's I going to get a thousand quid?!

Diana Start working.

Ketchum (*suddenly clutches his chest*) It's the ticker. Dropping behind enemy lines at Arnhem didn't help . . . hanging by a thread . . . lights down, curtain, the end.

Diana Stop play-acting.

Ketchum   We'd both look right Charlies if I stopped
play-acting. Besides, it hurts the same, play-acting or no.
(*He develops a limp.*) But I don't ask for sympathy. Don't
worry, it's nothing.

Diana   That's what I thought.

Ketchum   I'll show you what loving means! (*He grabs
the knife he stole.*) Now you're sorry. I'm going – it's the
only way.

*Plunges knife into his chest, which it doesn't even penetrate
his coat: he yells to the kitchen.*

Get yer bloody knives sharpened, they wouldn't cut
butter!

*As **Diana** watches exasperated, **Ketchum** grabs the cord
from **Aylmer**'s dressing-gown and ties the end in a noose
round his neck.*

Ketchum   Think I'm ripe for the funny-house, eh? Just
wait! Goodbye, Charlie! *Arrrr!* (*He tightens the noose.*)
Too late, another good man done dirty by a cold biddy.

*He scrambles up onto the table. **Diana** shouts into the
kitchen.*

Diana   Michael!

***Aylmer** and **Joan** are already coming in with a tea-tray.
They see **Ketchum** on the table trying to tie the end of the
cord to the light fixture.*

Aylmer   Charlie!

Joan   Don't scratch that table!

Ketchum   *Arrhhh!*

*Losing his balance **Ketchum** falls off with a crash.
Aylmer and **Diana** rush to help him whilst **Joan** anxiously
examines the table for scratches.*

Aylmer   What are you playing at now?

Ketchum   Yous bloody blind as well as stupid, I'm
hanging meself that's what I'm playing at. The greatest

man ever to pass through Bournemouth, turned down by a piece of ice-cold-nifty!

He charges away, bursting through the French windows. As he staggers onto the balcony to jump, **Aylmer** *grabs the trailing end of the neck cord and jerks him back. They fall in a heap.* **Ketchum** *is first up.*

Ketchum (*loosening noose*) You trying to strangle me?! You can't, mister, better men have tried – knives, guns, tanks, bombs, war and pox – I've licked 'em all. Still full of piss and ginger . . . Now, where was I? Oh yes . . . (*About to plunge onto balcony again, he sees the tea-tray.*) Ah, time for tiffin. I'm feeling peckish. It's funny how you don't notice when you're busy . . . (*Wolfs sandwich.*) Stale cheese! I told you afore about stale mousetrap. I prefer toasted marshmallows. I'd better stoke up hearty, 'cause I'm killing myself and then I'm leaving . . .

Blackout.

Scene Eight

'Our Love Is Here To Stay' is played softly in the darkness.

Spot up on **Joan** *and* **Aylmer** *on the sofa.*

Aylmer Have you noticed how quiet it is here, now?

Joan I didn't think he was actually going.

Aylmer Well, we won't forget him, and there aren't many people you can say that about.

Joan *gets up and switches up the volume on the radiogram so 'Our Love Is Here To Stay' is played a little louder.* **Aylmer** *crosses to her and they dance.*

As they do, spot up, Stage Right on **Ketchum** *in his old coat, crouching behind a glowing brazier, drinking with* **Gaff**, **Smith** *and* **Zacchaeus**.

Ketchum   Cold! The leaves are turning brown on the
Holyhead Road. She didn't want me but I was wanted at
Tobruk and the Ardennes, wasn't I?! Money! Gazuma!
That's the reason. Why are they warm and we're
shivering? Why are they snuggy-safe and we have to piss
in the dark? Why are they fat and the wind blows us over?
. . . (*They straighten up, their shadows grow bigger.*) It's
going to change! Haul up the black flag, boys, we're
sailing in with knives a'tween our teeth. We're going to
get our share! We'll make 'em weep! We'll make 'em
crawl! We'll make 'em eat shit! A million flies can't be
wrong . . .

Ketchum *and* **Others**, **Joan** *and* **Aylmer** *sing
simultaneously.*

Ketchum ⎫ (*singing*) 'May the bleeding piles assail you /
Others ⎭ From your head down to your feet / May
crabs the size of elephants / Crawl up your
balls and eat / And when you're old and
withered / And a syphilitic wreck / May you
fall down your own arse hole / And break
your bloody neck . . .' (*They howl.*)

Joan ⎫ (*singing*) 'Our Love Is Here To Stay'.
Aylmer ⎭

Spots out but **Ketchum** *and his companions continue
howling in the darkness.*

Scene Nine

Lights up on the living-room with **Ketchum**, **Gaff**, **Smith**
and **Zacchaeus** *slouching, and pawing the furniture
drunkenly.* **Ketchum** *lurches to the cocktail cabinet and
starts pouring drinks.*

Ketchum   Welcome to Piss-Pot Hall.

Gaff   Five years minimum sentence. One third remission for good conduct. Breaking into a dwelling-place is a serious offence between the hours of nine p.m. and six a.m. I know, I went bust.

Ketchum   Who's breaking in? I'm a Clubhouse guest here and have been for days. (*Holds up door key.*) Knew where this was, didn't I? (*Holds up bottle.*) And this – 'quid pro quo'. Don't stand there bleeding at the gills, smile, it's free drinks all round.

Gaff   No such thing as free drinks, free parking or free love either. I've always had to pay for 'em all, one way or the other.

Smith   Nnnnnnnn . . . ask Aggie. No orders. Off limits. Sign says, 'KEEP OUT'.

Zacchaeus   I've only had cold tea, cigarette-ends and stale boot-polish sandwiches for dinner, but dat booze ain't ours.

Ketchum   No, it's mine, but if you lot don't want it?

Others   We wouldn't say dat!

They grab the drinks.

Ketchum   Take off yer socks, this is Easy Street. (*Pulls Zacchaeus over to the bust.*) I come back for my old comrade Pie-Face Pearson. Old Flannel-Mouth says this is some hairy cock-chaser name of Bernie Ruskinsky. Now, does he look like Bernie Ruskinsky?

Zacchaeus   Looks more like Barney Rubin who used ta' play 'Ireland Must Be Heaven 'cause Me Mother Comes From There' on the silvers.

Ketchum   Looks like a lot of people, come to that. Sir James Ruskin the Harp Dealer, Basil Banta one o' the four Banta Brothers, Will Mahoney who danced on top of a xylophone with the hammers tied to his toes. (*Putting bust on sofa.*) It even looks a bit like Bert Russell.

Gaff My place was like this before the Lituanians got to work. Reduced my house to dust in Plumstead. Freehold property. Recently decorated throughout. Seventy-five per cent mortgage. Ring evenings only.

Smith (*stroking furniture*) Good married quarters. Aggie and me years ago. Lights out . . . good stuff . . .

Ketchum It's Jappo hardboard, riddled with woodworm, wood-weevil and dry rot!

He lashes out at the table leg. It splinters off and the table falls over. The others stare in horror.

Zacchaeus Dat's broken and we'll get blamed!

Ketchum We'll get thanked for it. I just saved 'em from a nasty accident. Suppose they were having a heavy dinner on it, slurping up mulligatawny soup when *crack*, that leg drops off sudden like?

Zacchaeus Dat's true, mulligatawny soup's a terrible staining thing.

Ketchum We've saved 'em. (*Pushing* **Gaff** *to a cane chair.*) Get up there! . . . (**Gaff** *climbs up, bottle in hand.*) Now jump! (**Gaff** *jumps.*) Harder! (**Gaff** *jumps harder and goes through the seat.*) Wood-weevil!

Zacchaeus (*staring at a print on the wall*) Birds have a cunning all their own. (*Takes down the print.*) I had a budgie once called Chico. If it hadn't been for Chico I'd've gone mad back in '51. (*Thrusts his fist through print.*) Chico . . . Chico . . . Chico . . .

Smith *has taken a book from the shelf and is staring at it reverentially.*

Smith B-B-B-Books. Queen's Regulations. Charge sheets. Orders. Words better than bullets . . .

Having disentangled himself from the chair, **Gaff** *crosses and takes the book from him. He opens it and removes his hat in respect.*

Gaff Words get into the mind sideways with knives. There's nothing like 'em. Words like . . . 'constipation' . . . 'bankruptcy' . . .

Zacchaeus 'Custard' . . . And what about 'knees'? Dat's a beautiful word, 'knees', 'K-n-e-e-e-e-e-e-s' . . .

Smith 'Halt' . . . 'Daphne' . . . 'figs' . . . 'bugger' . . .

Gaff I lost 'cause words were against me. Words, make a man humble.

Ketchum Makes a man pig-sick! (*Grabs book.*) Words is nothing, words is hot air, words is black marks on white paper! Words ain't real. (*Reads book's title.*) 'Plays of Sheikspear' . . . Sheikspear! Bloody Arab pen-pusher!

Zacchaeus He wrote plays hundreds of years ago, even before de Valera came to Ireland.

Ketchum Words don't frighten me none, they're all in the mind, when I crack the whip they jump . . . 'Marmalade' . . . Eh?! . . . 'Jock-strap' . . . Ha-ha-ha! . . . 'Chipping Norton' . . . Back, you dogs, back! . . . See, they know who's boss. (*Hits book.*) Words are used to keep us down, out and helpless – you gotta fight back. (*He tears the book in half: it lets out a scream of pain as pages fall out.*) It's nowt. Falling to pieces, no spine. All loose and fluttering. See, I'm the only one with spunk! And why! (*Singing.*) 'Cause my name is Charlie Ketchum, I'm the leader of the band, / And though we're small in number, we're the best in all the land. / Oh I am the conductor and we often have to play, / With all the best musicianers you hear about today!'

Zacchaeus, **Smith** *and* **Gaff** *fall in behind him singing and marching round the room, stamping over furniture and breaking ornaments.*

All (*singing*) 'When the drum go bang, and the cymbals clang, the horns will blaze away. / Gunboat plucks the old banjo, while Gaff the sax will play. / Oh Zackery, Zackery, tootles the spoons, my word it's something

grand. / Oh a credit to old England boys, is Charlie
Ketchum's band.'

Joan   My God!

They had been too busy singing to notice **Joan** *had entered.*
Upstage Right.

Ketchum   Surprise, surprise, Charlie's back. Meet
Gregarious Gaff from Plumstead; Zac-Zacchaeus – Irish
turncoat and lickspittle; Gunboat Smith – bronze medal,
Burma Star, Dishonourable Discharge.

Smith   Gi' us a fag, lady.

Joan   What've you done?!

Smith   Gi' us a fag, lady.

Joan   I'll give you the police!

Gaff
Zacchaeus } The rozzers!
Smith

They stampede away, flattening **Joan** *in their panic-stricken*
flight and exit Upstage Right.

Ketchum   Come back here, the party's just started!

Joan   Did you do this?

Ketchum   Thought you'd be pleased.

Joan   Pleased!?

Ketchum   Rickety stuff, blown together with spit and
wind.

Joan   You maniac!

Ketchum   Dropped a clanger, have I? All it needs is a
woman's touch.

Joan   I'll give you a woman's touch!

She hits him.

Ketchum Don't, missus, my head's splitting. There's little green men in size twelve galoshes . . . *Oooooh.* (**Joan** *grabs the phone.*) What you doing now, then?

Joan Getting the police.

Ketchum The screws! There's gratitude. I'm off.

He picks up the bust.

Joan Put that back! It's mine!

Joan *tries to pull the bust away from him.*

Ketchum Hands off! You don't happen to have a raw egg on you, hair of the dog? . . . My head, *oooh* . . .

Joan You thieving imbecile, give it to me!

He pulls the bust away from her and crashes into the TV which accidentally turns on.

Ketchum Shout softer, missus.

Joan (*kicking his shins*) Gimme!

Ketchum Dirty play, ref.

Joan Gimme!

Ketchum Take it then!

In a sudden rage, he hits her over the head with the bust.
Joan *topples to the floor bringing the standard lamp down with her, and knocks her head hard against the ground. Now the only light in the room is from the TV where we can see* **Aylmer**'s *face on the screen.*

Ketchum Now you'll have a thick head, same as me. (*Looks at shattered bust.*) Poor old Pie-Face, Rest In Pieces. I wouldn't lay there, missus, there's a draught up your knickers. (*Bends over and touches her.*) Missus, missus, you're scaring Charlie. Didn't mean no harm. What about a bit of a singsong, then? (*Falls on his knees beside her.*) Say something, missus. Don't hold your breath, people'll think you're dead. People don't know Charlie wouldn't knock the skin off a rice pudding . . . I didn't mean nothing, only jossing . . . Scarper! Face it,

Charlie, you're a hero with coward's legs, scarper! . . .
(*He scrambles up.*) No, your name's Charles Horatio
Ketchum, not Windy Willy. You gotta stay fer her sake.
Stiff upper, face the music, old soldiers never. Only one
life to give. Duty. (*Whips out medals and pins them on his
chest.*) It's the right thing to do, Charlie, but why is the
right thing always so bloody hard, and the wrong thing
always so bleedin' easy? *Oooh*, I'm scared . . .

*He picks up the phone and dials a number and speaks
unnaturally loud into the receiver.*

Hello, this is Mr Charlie Ketchum . . . I've just killed
somebody . . . yes, murder . . . crime of passion . . . This
is Fleet Street 3130 ain't it? 'Screws of the World'
newspaper? . . . Good . . . cause I'm selling you the whole
story for one thousand quid. Cash. And worth every
penny!

The TV sound comes on.

Aylmer's voice . . . From a seat in the Gods
everything that happens on earth provokes laughter. If
you're far enough away even the fight to the death
between two human beings can be funny. We only see
their absurd tumbles and not their contorted faces or
strangled cries. It's all a question of distance . . .

Exasperated, **Ketchum** *smashes the TV set.*

Scene Ten

Sound of a **Judge** *rapping his gavel for silence in the
darkness.*

Lights up on the courtroom. The **Judge**'s *rostrum is
Downstage Right with the* **Clerk of the Court**'s *desk below
it. Immediately to the left of him is the witness-box.*

Judge Members of the jury, the time for me to instruct
you in law is after you've heard the evidence. However,

you may have formed some opinion about the prisoner
due to the publicity he had received. But remember, you
must try this case solely on the evidence. The evidence
and nothing but the evidence must influence you for or
against the prisoner.

Ketchum Only the evidence? That don't seem fair.
There's other things to consider. What about this? (*Shows
his medals.*) And this?

*He jumps on chair, shows rolled-up trouser leg and points
triumphantly to his bare knee.*

Judge Don't interrupt! (**Ketchum** *scrambles down.*)
You are on trial for your life. For reasons best known to
yourself you have elected to stand trial without
counsel . . .

Ketchum No need, British justice's the best in the
world. No case too small, no fee too large!

Judge That is your privilege. But though I will allow
you every latitude, you have been informed of the correct
judicial procedure, so we will tolerate no behaviour which
lowers the dignity of this court.

Ketchum Dignity of the court . . . mmm . . . ipso facto
– bona fide – locus pocus . . . must have dignity.

Judge Ms Trevor, you may proceed.

Ms Trevor QC *rises ceremonially and tugs at her gown.
Throughout her speech* **Ketchum** *mimes to the audience, not
to take her seriously.*

Trevor QC May it please, my Lord, members of the
Jury, I appear in this case with my learned friend Mr
Day, for the prosecution. This is a case of murder in the
act of theft. Out of kindness, the deceased's husband,
Michael Aylmer, brought the prisoner home on the 12th
September, but due to his behaviour he was asked to leave
on the 13th. That same evening, with three accomplices,
he broke into Aylmer's flat. Mrs Aylmer surprised them,
and the three accomplices fled. I will show that the

prisoner then killed Mrs Aylmer with a blow from a
plaster bust of Bertrand Russell. The prisoner was later
that evening picked up by the police. He had on him an
alarm clock, a scrubbing-brush, a musical toilet-roll, two
pairs of stockings, eight spoons, cigarette-lighter, a silver
mousetrap and a giant packet of 'DAZ' washing-powder.
All items were identified as coming from Aylmer's house.
Mr Aylmer is suffering from a nervous breakdown and is
unable to testify at this time, but his signed statement will
be called in evidence. You will hear how after this hideous
crime the prisoner rang the Editor of the *News of the
World* and offered to sell his story. After concluding the
deal, the editor finally informed the police. The prisoner's
behaviour may predispose you to question his sanity . . .

Ketchum   'Ere, hold hard, that's a bit thick and juicy.

Trevor QC   But I will bring evidence to prove he knew
exactly what he was doing. We are dealing, members of
the Jury, with a brutal, cold-blooded, diabolically clever
murderer.

Ketchum   And handsome to boot.

Trevor QC   I call Detective Inspector Poole.

Clerk   Call Detective Inspector Poole.

As **Poole** *enters Upstage Right* **Ketchum** *grows agitated
and shoots up his hand.*

Judge   You have an objection?

Ketchum   Yes, me learned arse-crawler over there's
had her say, now it's my turn, fair does. British justice the
best in the world. (*Puts on a torn gown and claps a hideous
orange clown's wig onto his head.*) M'Lud, I would ask
m'Lud to take eighty-nine thousand similar cases under
consideration to whit . . . (*He tugs at his gown, which
tears.*)

Judge   Remove that ridiculous wig! (**Ketchum** *takes off
the wig.*) You will behave yourself. You will be given a

chance to speak after the Prosecution has put its case. Is that understood?

Ketchum Mal dicket, mal docket.

Judge Proceed, Ms Trevor.

Detective Inspector Poole *goes into the witness-box and takes up the oath card and Bible.*

Poole I swear by Almighty God that the evidence I shall give shall be the truth, the whole truth and nothing but the truth. Robert Poole, Detective Inspector, CID, New Scotland Yard.

Ketchum New Scotland Yard, members of the jury! Make a note of that word 'new'. 'Nough said . . .

Trevor QC I must object to these interruptions, m'Lud.

Judge Quite so, Ms Trevor. The prisoner will refrain from interrupting.

Trevor QC Inspector, please tell us what happened on the 13th September last?

Poole (*reading from notebook*) I received a call from Mr Michael Aylmer at 11.57 p.m. and proceeded to 31 Hampstead Way where I found Mrs Joan Aylmer dead from head wounds . . .

Ketchum I object!

Judge On what grounds?

Ketchum I don't like what he's saying.

Judge Objection over-ruled.

Ketchum Content.

Poole Whilst questioning Mr Aylmer I received a call from the editor of the *News of the World* newspaper who told me Charles Ketchum had confessed to the murder of Joan Aylmer.

Ketchum I don't object!

Judge You don't?

Ketchum Thank you, m'Lud.

Judge Er yes . . . the witness may continue.

Poole The prisoner was arrested at 1.25 a.m. and was formally cautioned.

Ketchum It's a lie, but I still don't object!

Trevor QC What did the prisoner reply on being so cautioned?

Poole (*consulting notes*) 'Ahhhh, you're breaking my arm, Flatfoot!'

Ketchum I know you! You're *Potty* Poole, got thrown off the Force – sticky fingers, on the take. Support the boys in blue, bribe a copper today!

Judge The prisoner will control himself, or will be forcibly restrained!

Ketchum It's Potty Poole! I'd know that bald spot and dandruff anywhere.

Trevor QC Your Lordship, I must protest.

Judge Quite so, Ms Trevor. But I said I'd give the prisoner some latitude as this is a capital charge . . . (*To* **Ketchum**.) However, you are abusing my indulgence. Strict rules of procedure are laid down in a Court of Law. They will be obeyed!

Ketchum But it's him. Fraudulent conversion, habitual prostitution, Rex-v-Damp, Gimble and Garland, 1949.

Judge Will you be silent!

Ketchum Mal dicket, mal docket, still say he's Potty Poole.

Judge Pray continue, Ms Trevor.

Trevor QC Detective Inspector, did the prisoner make a statement?

Poole No, he refused.

Trevor QC Why?

Poole (*reading notes*) He said he's already signed a contract with the *News of the World* and they were paying him one thousand pounds for his story. He wasn't interested in other offers. One thousand pounds was all he needed. Besides, he said, the police wanted it for free.

Trevor QC Thank you, Inspector.

Judge Do you wish to examine the witness, Mr Ketchum?

Ketchum Wouldn't examine him with a ten-foot pole and rubber gloves.

Judge You may step down, Inspector.

Poole *stands down and exits Upstage Left.*

Trevor QC I now call Joseph J. Gaff.

Ketchum Is he the same as Joe Gaff Esquire? Lockjaw Joe? Is it Lockjaw Joe?

Gaff *enters Upstage Right, goes into the witness-box and takes up the oath card and Bible.*

Gaff I swear by Almighty God that the evidence I shall give shall be the truth, the whole truth and nothing but the truth. Joseph J. Gaff of no fixed abode and then some.

Trevor QC Will you tell the jury, in your own words, Mr Gaff, about the events of the evening of the 13th September last.

Gaff The 13th. I had a bad day, the messages weren't coming through loud and clear. I suspected the Lituanians had been at it again . . .

Trevor QC The 13th of September please?

Ketchum What happened on the 13th?

Trevor QC I'm asking Mr Gaff.

Ketchum He doesn't talk to Lituanians.

Gaff   No, I never talk to Lituanians.

Trevor QC   I'm not Lituanian. I was born in
Shepherds Bush.

Ketchum   That's *your* story.

Judge   Will you get on with it!

Trevor QC   Mr Gaff, what happened on the evening of
the 13th September?

Gaff   Charlie Ketchum told us it'd be all right. But I
should've listened to the voices. I'm wired you know. Sir,
sir, don't send me back. I served my sentence. Nothing
more to give . . .

Trevor QC   Thank you, Mr Gaff.

Gaff *stands down and exits Upstage Left.*

Ketchum   *Comme ci, comme ça.* I rest my case.

Judge   You have something to say, Mr Ketchum?

Ketchum   Nuff said. British Justice. Oil and water
don't mix.

Trevor QC   Call Norman Zacchaeus.

Ketchum   Who's this one? I don't know no Norm Zach.
You spring 'em on me, like there was no tomorrow.

Zacchaeus *enters Upstage Right and goes into the witness-
box, takes up the oath card and Bible and makes the sign of
the cross over himself.*

Zacchaeus   I swear by Almighty God, the Father, Son
and Holy Ghost that the evidence I shall give shall be the
truth, the whole truth and nothing but the truth. Norman
Zacchaeus, Dublin Town. I'm Irish you know, broke
both my ankles making coconut wine.

Trevor QC   Mr Zacchaeus, will you please tell the jury,
in your own words, about the events of the 13th
September.

Zacchaeus   That was the day Charlie took us to his friends. Jaysus, gi' us a drink, mister. We all went to this friend of his, Mr Willy Aylmer so he said. Then he started taking things. Him not me, we Irish is law-abiding folk.

Trevor QC   Go on, Mr Zacchaeus.

Zacchaeus   Then the missus came back and Charlie starts quarrelling. We scarpered.

Trevor QC   The Missus? Mrs Aylmer?

Ketchum   You knew her too, did you? She knew her too, your Lordship. I think the case is pretty plain now.

Judge   No, she didn't know Mrs Aylmer. Did you, Ms Trevor?

Trevor QC   Well actually, I did. I met her once socially . . . But what has that to do with the case, your Lordship?

Judge   Nothing! Please continue, Ms Trevor.

Trevor QC   So you and your friends, Joseph Gaff and George Smith, under the leadership of the prisoner broke into Mr Aylmer's house and when Mrs Aylmer came in unexpectedly you, Smith and Gaff left leaving the prisoner arguing with Mrs Aylmer?

Zacchaeus   Sure, that's the story. Just ask de Valera.

Trevor QC   Thank you, Mr Zacchaeus. Mr Ketchum.

Ketchum   I'm not talking to him, he's Irish.

Judge   You may stand down, Mr Zacchaeus.

Ketchum   How can he stand down? Stand up, stand easy, stand ready, but stand *down*? Never!

Judge   I will not warn the prisoner again!

Ketchum *crouches and grovels.* **Zacchaeus** *comes out of the witness-box and exits Upstage Left.*

Trevor QC   Call George T. Smith.

Gunboat Smith *marches in Upstage Right, salutes the* **Judge**, *marches up into the witness-box.*

Smith Attention!

He comes to attention in the witness-box and stamps so hard he goes through the wooden floor. **Smith** *pulls himself up.*

Judge Are you all right, Mr Smith?

Smith All present and correct, sir! Reporting for duty . . . (*He takes up the oath card and the Bible.*) I, George T Smith, number 2487640, first class, dishonourable discharge, swear . . .

Ketchum Are you going to listen to a man who spent his life digging holes and filling them in again before setting light to his clothes?

Smith I never set light to my clothes.

Ketchum Gaff, Zacchaeus, now you! Even a cockroach wouldn't stab his own father in the back and that's what I've been to you lot – a father. The least you can do is *lie*, that's what friends are for!

Judge Mr Ketchum!

Ketchum The one and only. I can honestly claim, your Honour, to have made love more times than anyone else in the Western Hemisphere and I can make it stand up in court.

Judge I won't warn you again.

Ketchum No. Absolutely. But 'ave ya got a pot for a pee?

Judge This is a Court of Law!

Ketchum And this is a law of nature, your Grace. Beats all your other laws every time.

Judge I've never seen such gross contempt!

Ketchum Gross! You hairless, arse-'ole! Dressed up like a Mayfair ponce . . . Ladies and gents of the jury, I done nothing wrong else I'd know it. I was tight as a newt that night. You ain't topping an old soldier for that!

Judge Warder!

Ketchum *jumps viciously at the advancing* **Warder**, *sending him careering out of the dock.*

Ketchum   I got me rights. (*To* **Judge**.) You bald-headed, tit-faced, dried-up old fart – call this British justice?! (*Takes off boot and hurls it at the* **Judge**, *then amidst uproar grips the ledge of the dock and sings defiantly.*) 'Who are the yeomen, the freemen of England! / Stout were the bows they bore, / When they went out to war. / Stouter their courage for the honour of England!' . . .

Two **Warders** *finally prise him away, still singing and taking the dock ledge with them.*

Ketchum   'And Nations to eastward, nations to westward, as foremen did curse them, / The Bowmen of England! No other land can nurse them! / But their Motherland, old England! / And on her broad bosom will they ever thrive!'

He is finally dragged out. The court is in uproar.

Clerk   Order in the court! Order in the court! *Please* . . .

The **Judge**, *minus his wig, reappears nervously from behind his chair, with* **Ketchum**'s *old boot. He raps for silence, but the uproar continues. The* **Clerk** *points to the* **Judge**'s *bald head. The* **Judge** *suddenly realises he is without his wig, and searches behind his chair. He reappears almost immediately with his wig on. This time he sits, raps loudly, and the courtroom instantly becomes silent.*

Judge   Never before, in twenty-five years on the bench, have I had the misfortune to witness such a blatant exhibition of hooliganism from a prisoner. The court will adjourn to appoint counsel on his behalf, as it is obvious he is not competent to defend himself. Before adjourning, however, I have this to say to the jury. This vulgar display by the prisoner must not influence you. Only the evidence is relevant. You must not take into consideration his blasphemy, his obscenity, or even his murderous, unprovoked attack on me. For remember . . . (*The lights dim to a spot on the* **Judge**.) . . . as long as civilisation continues, British justice will remain the admiration of the world because of the inflexible honesty of its jury system and the scrupulous impartiality of its judges. I have no doubt that you, twelve good men and true, will reach a verdict which will be in keeping with the best traditions of an English Court of Law . . .

Spot up on **Ketchum**, *standing in the dock between two burly* **Warders**.

Charles Ketchum, the jury have, solely on the evidence presented, found you guilty of a singularly revolting crime. It is therefore my duty to pass upon you the only sentence known by law for such an offence . . .

As the **Judge** *solemnly puts on the traditional black cap and pronounces sentence,* **Ketchum** *points at him and sings as lights slowly out.*

Ketchum (*singing*)   'Where did you get that hat / Where did you get that tile? / Isn't it a nobby one and just the proper style? / I should like to have one just the same as that! / Where 'ere I go, they shout hello! / Where did you get that hat!'

Lights out.

Judge's voice   The evidence of the law upon you is that you be taken to a lawful prison and there to a place of execution. That you there be hanged by the neck until you be dead, and that your body be buried within the precincts of the prison in which you have been confined before execution. And may the Lord have mercy on your soul.

Act Two

Scene One

A conference room, 1990. **Gerald Woods**, **John Euston** *and* **Norman Stoner** *are seated at a table. The chair at the top end of it is turned facing Upstage. Door Stage Right.*

Woods I will dispense with the reading of the minutes of the last meeting and come directly to the business in hand. Gentlemen, according to all the latest reports, the situation is worse than we thought possible.

Stoner Tokyo Nikke Index down 193.50 to 26249.02. Frankfurt DAX Index down 24 points to 1658.39. Hong Kong is looking sick and London is closed for the day. That says it all, Mr Woods.

Euston There was a big sell overhang from individuals who brought on margin and liquidated their holdings so today's 8% rebound in shares means nothing when the market turnover needs to be 60% higher according to Phillips Draught Shawcross & Weights.

Woods What're we going to do about it? Have you any suggestions, Mr Chairman?

The chair at the top of the table turns to reveal **Ketchum**. *He is that much older, his hair and beard are now white and trimmed, and he has on a dark jacket and tie.*

Ketchum Gentlemen, I've been sitting here thinking knowledge sucks and wisdom dribbles. I've served the company over thirty years . . . Where've they gone? Who's got them? . . . In the beginning I was wild, bit of a rough diamond. But I stayed on, trimmed the gardens, wound the clocks and ended up chairman of the whole caboodle. Now I'm yellowing at the edges, I sag and droop, croak and creak. There's cold in my veins and I never get warm. I thought now some of my pep's gone I'd pick up my bag and travel on, retire to Eastbourne or the hanging gardens of Holyhead. But it's one fight more it seems. Least I can do after what this organisation's done for me. We've got to act and scotch the rumours. First, we get the British public on our side. In a fight like this you need all the support you can get, however unsavoury. So I propose to make a press statement. I've taken the liberty, as I always will, of drafting out a statement, pro tem. It's short and to the point. (*Despite his eye-patch he puts on a pair of glasses, produces a piece of paper and reads.*) Statement issued 1st July 1990 by the Chairman, Mr Charles Ketchum. 'Bolt the doors, nail down the windows, block the chimneys, thieves are coming to clean out the store. I think that sums it up nicely.

The others thump the table in approval as **Dr Burgess** *enters Stage Right in a white overall carrying thick files.*

Dr Burgess　What're you patients doing in the conference room? I asked you to come to my office.

Euston, Stoner *and* **Woods** *scramble up.*

Woods　Just practising our parts pro and con as elected representatives of 'D Wing' Mentals, Dr Burgess.

Ketchum *gets up to show he is dressed in pyjama trousers and plimsolls.*

Ketchum　Wait a minute. I used to know an eminent MD who looked exactly like you called Dr Nathanial Burgess. Any relation?

Dr Burgess　I am Nathanial Burgess.

Ketchum　No wonder you look like him. But I still insist there is a resemblance.

Dr Burgess　Because I *am* Nathanial Burgess.

Ketchum　That accounts for it! We've come about the rumours, Doctor Nat. Word has it they're closing 'D Wing' and we nutters're being moved on to other loony bins. Is that the right, left or centre of it?

Dr Burgess Almost right. We have to implement new government policy. 'D Wing' is being closed but you're not going to other institutions. You're going back into the community. It's called community care. The majority of you're being discharged.

Euston *falls on his knees,* **Woods** *trembles violently,* **Stoner** *drops his trousers and* **Ketchum** *sits slowly, takes off his glasses and cleans them revealing they have no lenses as he pulls a dirty handkerchief through the frames.*

Stoner Discharged? But I don't discharge any more now. Holding it back. If I once let go and discharged all my urine I'd flood the world. I have to contain it in me whatever the cost otherwise I'd drown millions . . .

Euston The hordes're waiting for me if I leave. Women'll pluck it out by the roots. I must go. Marie Antoinette's my control and she's getting impatient. If I'm late she might lose her head.

Woods I don't understand. I've always been grateful I'm in a fully heated building. I'm the sort who'd send out for pizzas if I knew how.

Dr Burgess Choices have to be made and I have to make them. Time for your medication. You stay, Mr Ketchum.

Dr Burgess *guides* **Stoner,** **Woods** *and* **Euston** *to the door and they exit. He then joins* **Ketchum** *at the table.*

Dr Burgess Mr Ketchum, the staff think you should remain under custodial care. They have grave fears – not for you but the public at large. (*He opens the largest file.*) This is all you. Sentenced to death for murder '65, reprieved at the last moment because hanging was repealed, sent to Broadmoor, and moved onto various psychiatric prison hospitals. They seemed to have tried everything on you from occupational therapy to exorcism. Pumped you full of every expensive drug they could think of just to keep you stable. Without much success it seems. I see you've been accused of attempted assault, indecent exposure and other acts of vandalism. But in the last few years – nothing. Have you grown too old to be dangerous, Mr Ketchum?

Ketchum If I were a dog I'd only be nine. After the trial I was booked for a week's engagement at the Crystal Room of the Cranley Inn Faversham, the Athens of the North. Instead, I've spent thirty odd years Rip Van Winkling in white rooms, jammed with thirty-foot needles and the stuff they slip into your tea: drugged to the eyeballs, Jeffrey. I've changed, instead of being wild and free, a beggar on the fly I've had to put my shoes on backwards and walk into myself. No chance of me going back into a world full of holes.

Dr Burgess You and the others have to learn to live it.

Ketchum Whaa? Whaa? You can't be thinking of sending me out with the others? Not me, not poor old Charlie. It's too late, Harold. I can't even walk round the boundaries of my mind now – I'm lost.

Dr Burgess Those recommended for discharge will have complete support systems to fall back on outside – full supplementary benefits, hostel accommodation, psychiatric and out-patient care and the rest.

Ketchum You're madder than I am! I've got a soft landing here. (*Falls on knees.*) I'm on me old prayer bones a-begging, leave me be. If you do I'll keep quiet. Your secret's safe with me. You're Dr Nathanial Burgess. *The* Dr Nathanial Burgess, the one who's been treating a man in 'E Wing' for yellow jaundice for fifteen years and only found out yesterday he was Chinese. (*He gets up.*) You're all alike! No listen, listen, we can come to some arrangement. I'm sure you're open to honest bribery like the rest of 'em. Just let me stay, sir, sir! I'll never get another snug like this.

Dr Burgess I'm sure you won't, Mr Ketchum. You have to face it, the government's policy is to combine maximum market profitability with minimum social responsibility, so mental disorder is no longer an excuse to free-load. Your behaviour has dispelled any doubts I may have had. I shall be recommending your discharge. You should've gone years ago.

Ketchum   No, I'm a poor old man. What's to become of me out there?

Dr Burgess   Get used to it, Mr Ketchum.

He exits leaving **Ketchum** *bent and shaking. But the moment the door shuts* **Ketchum** *straightens up and does an exhilarating tap dance round the room.*

Ketchum   Free! Free! Free at last! Out of the bottle and free! (*Singing.*) 'Laughing in a rainstorm. / Dancing in the snow. / Charlie's on the loose agin. / Just you watch him go. / All those well-scrubbed faces. / Sniggering behind my back. / Chop their rotten heads off. / Stretch 'em on the rack. / Blow away your worries. / Blow away your woes. / Good times round the corner. / Which one I'd like to know. / Laughing in a rainstorm. / Dancing in the snow. / Charlie's on the loose again. / Just you watch him go . . .' Ouch! Ahh! The more I said I was scared to go, the more Dr Kildare thought I was like the rest of 'em. But I'm not. It'll be the authentic come-back of Charles Horatio de Witt Ketchum, king of the kipper-houses. In a world of pygmies a giant returns. (*The lights go down imperceptibly.*) After thirty years I'll step out into the spotlight again . . .

A spot snaps on and he steps into it as **Euston**, **Woods** *and* **Stoner** *in coats and carrying battered suitcases appear out of the darkness behind him. They hand him his overcoat and trumpet. He blows a triumphant blast.*

Scene Two

Ketchum's *trumpet blast turns tremulous and plaintive as lights up on a cemetery and approaching storm. Heads bowed,* **Ketchum**, **Euston**, **Woods** *and* **Stoner** *stand shivering around a grave.*

Ketchum   England's dead, m'dear. They've turned mean with the years. I thought they'd set out flags to greet the return of the old battler. In the old days me and my kind were one-offs. Now there's thousands and thousands of mumbling bastards tramping the gutters of England. The Holyhead Road's jam-packed with shufflers and every spare spot is tramp-city. I chose the sky-blue life but this lot've been dropped straight into it. Walking on their knees to give their arches a rest. The years . . . the years . . . they've changed the world and me worse than all yer drugs. Made me soft. I'm out in the cold and the rain and the dark and not a bugger do I know. Oh Charlie . . . Oh Charlie . . . yer a poor lost loon . . .

Stoner   Where's the toilets? I used to know all the toilets in 'D Wing' even the ones they hid.

Euston   How can I make my fortune just standing around?

Woods   I don't understand why we're here? We should be snugged down in some hostel.

Ketchum   I'm here to pay my respects. This is the last resting-place of the woman I accidentally put under in my hot blood. Sorry there, lass. First thing I promised to do when I got out was to say I was sorry. Matter of honour. Forgive and forget a sick old man, sweet Joan in the starries.

Euston   You didn't tell us she was Jewish?

Ketchum   How do you know?

Euston   This is Golders Green Cemetery.

Ketchum   Yes, Jesus made her kosher . . . RIP sweet Joan, sweet Joan Aylmer.

Woods   Joan Aylmer? But this is the grave of a Mrs Sadie Rothschild.

Stoner   Well, it's the thought that counts.

Ketchum   Is nothing sacred?! It's grave robbers. Someone's been playing tricks on an old man! I want the

old times, the old faces. Can't cope. Zacchaeus, Joe Gaff
and Gunboat Smith sunk without a trace, all hands lost.
Where's the band I made into the finest heard this side
of Chingford? Banjo, sax and spoons and the golden
trumpet of C. Ketchum. You lads need a paying
profession and I'll show you how. Stoney, you can play
banjo. You look exactly like Gunboat Smith the virtuoso
of the strings.

Stoner I can't play nothing. I can't keep still long
enough.

Ketchum S'easy. You can be another Gunboat, just a
matter of practice. Gunboat was a soldier like me and he'd
say things like . . . (*He imitates* **Smith's** *voice*.) 'Poo pee
. . . eeee . . . 'es o' para' . . . sick parade . . . what 'appens
t'all, t'all, t'all the women? . . . they can't touch me . . .'
Now you say it.

Stoner Poo pee . . . eeee . . . 'es o' para' . . . sick parade
. . . what 'appens t'all, t'all, t'all the women? . . . they
can't touch me . . .'

Ketchum You're a natural! You'll be as good as
Gunboat on the banjo in no time. Just keep practising.
Woodsy you look the spitting image of Zacchaeus. It's the
spoons for you. He was a master of the silvers.

Woods Spoons! I can't play the market with spoons.

Ketchum Zacchaeus was Irish, that's the thing to
remember. Had an Irish way with cutlery. You'll soon
pick it up. Just keep saying . . . (*He imitates* **Zacchaeus'**
voice.) 'Plain jake's der stuff fer breakfast, just plain jake,
plain jake . . . Dirty sheets, cigarette burns, 344 out.'
Now it's your turn.

Woods 'Plain jakes the stuff for breakfast . . .'

Ketchum 'Plain jake's *der* stuff *fer* breakfast . . .' A
little more of the Irish if you please, Mr Woods. Just keep
at it and you'll have those spoons dancing.

Woods   'Plain jakes der stuff fer breakfast. Jus' plain jake . . .'

Ketchum   That's it! And last in line, the Gigli of the sax, old Joe Gaff. That's you, Euston, old son. You could be his twin. Now Gaff was wired and the Lituanians were always doing him down.

Euston   He sounds mad. Everybody knows there's nothing wrong with Lituanians. It's the Pomeranians you've got to watch.

Ketchum   If you want to play the sax like Joe Gaff it's gotta be the Lituanians. Now just follow old Joe . . . (*He imitates* **Gaff**'s *voice*.) 'I'm wired. My back teeth are wired. They send messages from beyond and further. That's how I get advanced warning about the Lituanians . . .' Right, you're on!

Euston   'I'm wired. My back teeth are wired. They send messages from beyond and further. That's how I get advanced warning about the Lituanians . . .'

Ketchum   Music to my ears. You'll soon be swinging that sax along with the best. See how easy it is being Gunboat, Zacchaeus and Joe Gaff and playing in a real band? Of course, we've got to get some instruments first but that's no problem. Just stick with Charlie, he'll see you right. Say goodbye to poor old Joan here. Last respects done with a bit of dignity. (*He salutes the grave*.) You're well out of it, m'dear . . . Now follow me. Keep practising lads, keep practising.

As he flourishes his trumpet they follow him in a line out of the cemetery whilst the lights go down.

Stoner	Poo' pee . . . eee . . . o' para . . . eeeee . . .
Woods	Plain jake's der stuff . . . der stuff . . . der stuff . . .
Euston	I'm wired . . . my back teeth are wired . . . wired . . .

They disappear in the darkness to the sound of rolling thunder.

Scene Three

The thunder turns into organ music. Lights up on a church and on a **Priest** *in the pulpit, Stage Right. The altar is Stage Centre and behind it a stained-glass window.*

Priest   Since Adam's fall all human beings have been living in a state of sin. God has therefore decreed that there should be inferior and superior social orders, a system guaranteed to cause an equal degree of suffering to all. True human freedom is to be found in man's ability to suffer humbly . . . (*He cannot see the figure of* **Ketchum** *coming quietly up the pulpit steps.*) We must continue believing in God's love despite all appearances to the contrary. We must practise humility and obedience, secure in the knowledge that He will reward us, one day.

Ketchum *pops up in the pulpit.*

Ketchum   That don't seem a very good bargain to me.

Priest   *Ahhhh!*

Ketchum   This is a bit of a tight squeeze, Father.

Priest   I'm in the middle of rehearsing my sermon – who the devil are you?! . . . Where's George?! How'd you get in? Where's Security?

Ketchum   Ketchum's the name.

Priest   Stop breathing in my face!

He tries to push **Ketchum** *out of the pulpit but they are jammed tight.*

Ketchum   Awkward time eh? . . . I can take a hint . . . If . . . ya just move . . . off . . .

Priest   George!

They struggle to disentangle themselves.

Ketchum   And you can get your hand off my inside leg I know all about that . . .

Priest   George!

He gives a tremendous heave sending both himself and
Ketchum *down the pulpit steps.* **Ketchum** *picks himself
up.*

Ketchum   Least now we can have a natter in peace.

Priest (*getting up*)   Who're you?

Ketchum   My card . . . (*He hands him a card which
concertinas out into about twenty, all shapes and sizes.*)
You're my support system.

Priest   Your what?

Ketchum   Support, support. I'm an old man and I need
all the support I can get. The padre, young Father
Padley, told us to look you up if we was in trouble, so did
Doc Burgess. If you're in trouble look in on St Margaret
on the Green.

Priest   Oh I see . . . The soup kitchen's outside in the
annex. Go see one of my staff, they deal with hand-outs
and charity work.

He starts to move off but **Ketchum** *pulls him back.*

Ketchum   I don't take charity unless it's free. No, this
is soul-work, your Grace. Now I'm getting old I have to
box crafty with the Governor Upstairs. I've gone a bit
spiritual.

Priest   Where's Security?! We hire Security just to keep
people like you out.

Ketchum   It's the killing I did you see . . .

Priest *stops struggling*.

Priest   Killing?

Ketchum   Put in the funny farm for it. Years of my life
down the toilet, like a dream. They did me dirt. I'm going
to look 'em up and have it out. I forgive 'em of course, but
I don't trust myself. Years of brooding, Father. Might do
something I shouldn't. Now my hairs are white I think of
the Governor Upstairs so I'd like to clear it with Him

beforehand just in case . . . I want you to give me absolution.

Priest   Give you what?

Ketchum   Absolution. That's the word Father Padley used. Now I'm not asking for absolution for something I've done but something I might do, understand.

Priest   I understand. But I can't give you absolution.

Ketchum   Why's that?

Priest   Because I'm not a Roman Catholic priest.

Ketchum   Why's that?

Priest   Because this isn't a Roman Catholic Church. The Archbishop may be besotted with the Ecumenical Movement but we are still staunchly Protestant. We do not believe in the pestilential Popish practices of incense, the confession of sins and hope for pardon. There is none.

Ketchum   Christ, I've buggered it up again.

Priest   I'll fight religious tolerance wherever I see it. It's just another name for weakness.

Ketchum   I used to be road-wise, knew my onions. Since I got out I don't know my arse from my elbow, Father.

Priest   I'm not your Father!

Ketchum   You could be if I was younger, my ma was fancy-free. I've got a question, Rev. Are the pearls on the Pearly Gates real? Worth a fortune. Over the years thoughts like that, escape from my head and I'd try to catch them. I didn't have anything better to do. I've got good thoughts now, I feel a prayer coming on.

He falls on his knees and drags the **Priest** *down beside him.*

Priest   Mr Ketchum, I've got work to do, I can't waste time praying.

Ketchum   It's this place. I feel peace and goodwill to all . . . Forgive and forget, turn the other cheek . . . Thirty years! . . . I could've been free and clear with my lovely, instead of being parboiled and roasted. I forgive 'em one and all. . . . Now I smile sweet, drugs and old age have turned me into a weasel-eyed, sponge-gutted, mushy-fisted, jelly-spined, yoghurt-eating old fool. Now I'd even smile sweet at Mr Know-It-All Aylmer who stole my life. He did! He did! . . . (*As he jumps up the* **Priest** *sidles away and exits.*) It's all his fault. He woke me up! I was sleeping and he woke me up! It'd've all been different if he hadn't woken me up! May his bones rot in Hell and his prong drop off! (*Singing.*) 'May your eyes go rheumy and your arse go slack. / May your dentures stink and your bridgework crack. / May you sweat and have scabs on all your pores. / May you have Bright's Disease and Bright have yours. / But most of all I pray you end up poor. / You hairy loathsome four-eyed bore.'

Lights snap out as the **Priest** *and two* **Security Guards** *rush in and dive at* **Ketchum**. *There is a tremendous crash and cry.*

Scene Four

A band plays 'Happy Birthday to You'.

Lights up on the terrace of **Aylmer**'s *country house on a starry summer's night. Stage Right french windows to the living-room. Stage Left an impression of trees.*

Michael Aylmer, *now with silver hair and a moustache is seated at a candlelit table with* **Peter Barnes**, *the writer.*

Aylmer   When Nietzsche wanted to scream his mother would stop his mouth with slices of apple which he chewed while growling softly to himself. I seem to have gone through my life growling softly and my mouth stuffed with bits of apple. I couldn't change the world so I gave up. What a mess.

Barnes You can't win. If you're too wise people will expect too much of you. If you're too conceited, you'll be thought obnoxious. If you're too humble you'll be overlooked. If too silent, ignored. If too hard you'll be broken. If too soft you'll be crushed. QED.

Aylmer You're a great comfort, Peter.

Barnes How can you be so sad on your birthday?

Aylmer It's the drink . . . the night . . . and the music.

Barnes You're a success. Michael Aylmer OBE; you've managed to turn television into an almost serious forum of debate, brought politics and art together and proved they're simply business by other means. Of course you've been very lucky.

Aylmer I've changed over the years, some say for the worse but at least I was trying to change. No longer. I've become a statue. I feel the pigeons shitting on my head. It's finished.

Barnes It's never finished, Michael. The stoics say whenever the planets return, to the same positions they had at the beginning of time, it produces universal destruction. But after everything is destroyed the cosmos is restored in precisely the same way as before. And the stars move in their courses exactly as before and Socrates and Plato, you, Michael Aylmer, and me, Peter Barnes, and every man and woman lives again with the same friends and enemies. They go through the same experiences and the same activities. Every city, street, field, sea, desert is restored as it was, to the last grain of sand and drop of water. And this restoration of the Universe takes place over and over again, time without end. So everything changes and nothing changes and there'll never be anything new, only that which has been before.

Aylmer It sounds like Hell.

A slight mist and the faint ragged sound of a band from the trees Stage Left. **Aylmer** *and* **Barnes** *turn in their chairs as the band grows louder playing 'Rolling Round the World', badly.*

Ketchum *emerges with a trumpet from the trees followed by* **Woods, Euston** *and* **Stoner** *in a line playing their instruments.* **Aylmer** *rises slowly as* **Ketchum** *ends the song with a shaky trumpet blast and salutes.*

Ketchum   'Allo, 'allo, 'allo. Guess who? Yes it's your old pal, mate and buddy, back from the dead, the one and only . . .

Aylmer   *Ahhhh!*

He faints and slumps to the ground.

Barnes   Michael!

He rushes over to him.

Ketchum   Was it something I said?

Woods   You said ''Allo, 'allo, 'allo'.

Euston   Maybe he's wired?

Stoner   Get him to the nearest toilet and quick.

Ketchum   Rubbish, get him into a cold bath, that'll bring him round.

Barnes *lifts* **Aylmer's** *head.*

Barnes   We'd better call for help . . . (*He gestures to the bottle on table.*) . . . The drink . . .

Ketchum   Good thinking . . . (*He picks up the bottle, takes a swig and passes it round.*) I feel better already.

Barnes   One of you, go for help!

Euston *wanders off towards the french windows Stage Right and peers in whilst* **Ketchum** *bends down beside* **Aylmer.**

Ketchum   Stick his head between his legs . . . I used to be a male nurse in a fever hospital. Charles Ketchum's the name and these are my professional colleagues. Virtuosos to a man. Who're you?

Barnes   Peter Barnes . . . Yes, let's try and get his head up.

Ketchum   Peter Barnes? You're joking. You're not *the* Peter Barnes? Peter Barnes the old scribbler?

Barnes   Yes . . . that's me.

Ketchum   We've met 'afore. You used to come to Broadmoor with that other gasbag, Sam Bucket, putting on plays for them that couldn't face life and liked pretending. Wait a minute, you sure you're *the* Peter Barnes, the real Peter Barnes? You don't look like him.

Barnes   I've never been to Broadmoor with Sam Bucket or anyone else but I am *the* Peter Barnes, the real Peter Barnes . . . Michael?! . . . Michael?!

Ketchum   You don't look like the real Peter Barnes. You're too smooth.

Stoner   You look too toilet-trained to me.

Woods   I've never met either Peter Barnes but I'd have to agree there's something wrong.

Ketchum   Most people wouldn't spot the deception. They don't know the real Peter Barnes. But I do. You're not a good enough likeness.

Barnes *jumps up angrily, letting* **Aylmer**'s *head fall back with a crash.*

Barnes   I don't know who you are, or you or you! But I know who I am. And I am *the* Peter Barnes, the real Peter Barnes, the one and only!

He grabs the bottle back from **Ketchum**, *kneels beside* **Aylmer** *and pours some drink into his mouth.*

Ketchum   All right, honest mistake. There's no need to lose your paddy.

Euston   We was just making polite conversation.

Aylmer *groans and opens his eyes.*

Barnes   Michael, are you all right? How do you feel?

He helps **Aylmer** *towards a chair.*

Aylmer   I must've drunk too much . . . I had a terrible nightmare.

Ketchum   No, that was me!

Aylmer   My God it's real!

As he collapses into the chair they do not notice a figure coming through the french windows. It is **Diana Bishop**, *years older, but still severely beautiful.*

Diana   Michael? . . . All the guests have gone . . . What happened?

Ketchum   It's my Di! Di my lovely it's your true love come home. 'Allo, 'allo, 'allo . . .

Diana *sees* **Ketchum** *for the first time.*

Diana   Ahhhh!

She slumps to the ground in a faint. They look at **Ketchum**.

Ketchum   What did I say? What did I say?

Woods   You said "Allo, 'allo, 'allo' again.

Barnes   Quick, someone help me.

He bends down beside **Diana** *with* **Woods** *who hands him the bottle.* **Barnes** *wets her lips.*

Ketchum   It's a miracle. She came for me. Me old Di's been waiting all these years. When they fall fer the likes of me, they stay felled. It's natural but I'm touched. Frankly I didn't expect it, but she's proved a good 'un . . . (**Diana** *groans and opens her eyes.*) Easy with her, lads. Easy, lads, easy. (**Barnes** *and* **Woods** *help* **Diana** *up into a chair.*) I was going to search the length and breadth of England for you. Now there's no need. We're together again like Cain and Abel, Murgatroyd and Winterbottom, never to be parted, hand in hand, my old Dutch, just you, me and the gatepost.

Barnes   This lady is Mrs Aylmer.

Ketchum   Mrs Aylmer?

Aylmer   She's my wife.

Ketchum   *Ahhh!*

He crashes to the ground in a faint. With a sigh **Barnes** *takes the bottle and bends down beside* **Ketchum**.

Woods   Is he out? He's not faking?

Barnes   Doesn't seem to be.

Euston   Now's our chance, lads. We can never get a word in edgeways when motor-mouth Charlie's up and doing. Quick, quick, we've got important things to say like, a gurk is not a swallow . . .

Woods   Me first, me first! You wouldn't think so looking at me now but I've been in love too. Young Mary Fitts – striking girl with a big nose. It used to fascinate me. I'd spend hours watching what she could do with it . . .

Stoner   Last summer I got pretty desperate about the state of the planet as if I didn't have enough problems of my own . . .

Woods   She'd use it to turn the pages of the hymn book in church, and she'd often go 'Sniff-sniff' and say 'There's someone cooking cabbage in Manchester'. One wedding reception we went to, she nodded and cut the cake with that nose by mistake . . .

Euston   Did you hear about the man who got this unsigned letter telling him to go to the local graveyard at midnight? He went but did he vote for Teddy Roosevelt in the 1904 Elections? . . .

Stoner   Life is like a train. If the station it gets you to is Brighton it's oysters and champagne. And if the station is some stop in Neasden with nothing to eat or drink and no toilet facilities, it's still your station. It's not my fault! I didn't lay the track or fix the schedules . . .

Diana and *Aylmer* *have recovered. Ignoring the others they stare at the slumped figure of* *Ketchum*.

Diana   Is it him?

Aylmer   It couldn't be anyone else.

Barnes   Will somebody explain? Who is he?

Aylmer   Nobody really . . . only the man who killed my first wife.

Diana   What are we going to do? Do you think he's escaped?

Woods   Escaped? No we was all booted out the same rest-home. Four sick hippos looking for a mud-bath. I'm Mr Woods known professionally as Zacchaeus. And this is Mr Stoner known as Gunboat Smith.

Euston   I'm Mr Euston working under de *nom de plume* of Joe Gaff.

Barnes   Irish? I'm going to phone the authorities! I've created too many monsters not to make sure I don't get within miles of 'em in real life.

He exits Upstage.

Woods   Authorities?! Not for us.

Stoner   Previous engagements you understand.

Euston   When Charlie wakes tell him we'll meet him under the clock somewhere or other.

They lift imaginary hats and exit fast Stage Left playing 'Rolling Round the World'.

Ketchum *groans faintly.*

Ketchum   Champagne . . . force champagne down my throat.

Aylmer   It can't be true, not after all these years.

Diana He's back like a bad dream.

Ketchum I just had a dream, Di. Terrible 'twas, the old ticker couldn't stand it. I dreamed you married Four-Eyes.

He drinks from the bottle.

Diana I did. I have.

Ketchum Say it isn't so! How could you? I remember last time we met I sang 'I'm shy little Di, I'm shy' and we talked of money and you said you was mine for a thousand. And when it all turned awkward you said you'd wait. But you couldn't, could you? You couldn't wait the odd thirty years. Oh no, you snapped up the first Tom, Mike or Harry that passed. Left poor old Charlie in the lurch.

Aylmer She never said she'd wait.

Ketchum I'm not speaking to you after what you did to me.

Aylmer What *I* did to *you*?! It was my wife you killed.

Ketchum Trust you to bring that up now . . . What you done with Gunboat and Zac and Irish Joe? Scarpered, have they? I must say you two look your age – guilt can do terrible things, Mike me lad. If it wasn't for you and your kind I'd've had a rich full life as layabout and lowlife. The years've put years on you, Di. You wouldn't've put on that double chin if you'd been on the road with me.

Diana Say something, Michael, even if it's only 'help'!

Aylmer If the authorities catch you here, Ketchum, you'll be for it. You haven't changed but we've changed, those who don't change don't grow.

Diana And we've grown tough.

Ketchum Yes, England's changed. I smelt it the moment I got out – stale piss and rot. Before I sang and danced and the wheat grew tall. Now look at it.

Everything's gone mean. That's another black mark against you, Mr Clever-Dick. You let it happen.

Aylmer   I let it happen?

Diana   Stop talking to him, Michael, and get him out!

Barnes *enters Upstage.*

Barnes   They should be here any minute.

Ketchum   This man is a fake! He could be Sliding Billy Watson, Bozo Schnyder or even Cheese 'n' Crackers Hogan but take my word for it he's not the author he says he is . . . Look, I've had a terrible day what with one thing and another, any chance of you putting up an old friend for the night?

Diana
Aylmer } Never!

Ketchum (*slumping down*)   Women have changed too. Now it isn't enough for a man just to be an idiot, they want more.

Barnes   Why do you say I'm not the real Barnes? Are there others out there?

Aylmer   Ketchum, you'd better go. The police'll be here any minute. I don't care about you but they might start digging up all the old stuff. I don't want to be involved in a scandal.

Ketchum   And I know why 'cause you've got something to hide. You don't want to lose what you've got. You lived soft and grabbed the glory. I hope you realise that when the Queen – God bless her and all who sail in her – says 'Rise Sir Peregrine Topaze Four-Eyes Aylmer, you've got your knighthood.'

Aylmer   How did you know I'm up for a knighthood?

Ketchum   I've got my sources – Branden de Vere, Knight Errant to the Royal Bedchamber had a cell next to mine.

Barnes I didn't know you'd been offered a title, Michael?

Diana No one does. He's only just been asked.

Aylmer I haven't accepted yet. I've always believed the English are an aristocracy-loving people, mesmerized by hocus-pocus, primogeniture and pageantry. But Diana wants it.

Ketchum You can't get a title just for yakking. I object.

Diana Nobody cares if you object or not, Ketchum. All we want from you is your absence. We've lived our lives, lives you don't know about, and now we want some peace.

Aylmer Wars, revolutions, gluts, famines, booms and busts, the world's moved on since you were out in it. There's nothing here for you, Ketchum. We won't let you in.

As **Aylmer, Diana** *and* **Barnes** *stare implacably at him there is the faint sound of ambulance and police sirens.*

Ketchum Aiii . . . aiii . . . It's the sound of all the broken lovers of the world . . .

Barnes No, that's the police and the ambulance. I called 'em both just to make sure.

The sirens grow louder.

Ketchum Why didn't somebody say?! We've been yakking here like there was no tomorrow . . . I've gotta hide . . . (*He starts to dive under the table but stops.*) No . . . that's the first place they'll look . . . I never panic except in a crisis . . . (*He zigzags about in increasing panic as the sirens grow louder and the lights fade down.*) Here . . . there . . . no . . . steady . . . I don't know the meaning of the word fear, terror yes . . . (*He slumps into a chair.*) I'll sit down and pretend I'm just a visiting nobody . . . No, they'd spot right off I'm a better class of person than they'd usually find here . . . (*He jumps up.*) What's a seven-letter word meaning goodbye? . . . Must run . . . can't . . . too old . . . stand still . . . pretend I'm invisible

. . . Help! . . . (*The sirens grow louder as he scrambles distraughtly up on the table.*) Yes . . . *eeeh* . . . *ahh* . . . *aiiii* . . . Somebody switch off the lights! . . .

He snaps his fingers and the light from the moon and stars is snapped off too as the screaming sirens finally drown out his frightened cries.

Scene Five

Spot up on **Diana** *in a double bed Stage Centre.* **Aylmer** *is sitting on the edge.*

Diana   I thought Barnes behaved like a twit.

Aylmer   He's a writer. He doesn't write about the world he sees when he opens his eyes but the world he sees when he closes them. So he's totally useless for all practical purposes.

Diana   What're we going to do about Ketchum?

Aylmer   I want him back inside, locked and bolted.

Diana   We made the mistake of believing because something that unpleasant happened once it couldn't happen again. It came back with him. What're you thinking about?

Aylmer   The mysteries of life . . . the hidden links that draw people together.

Diana   I'm looking at the veins between my fingers. I'm growing old, Michael . . .

Aylmer   It's all to do with time. Time can be given or taken away, kept or killed. There are old-timers and egg-timers, half-time, full time, short time and overtime. There's a time to be born and a time to die, a time to reap and to sow, good times, bad times, the best and worst of times, which waits for no man as it flies never to return . . .

Diana *is asleep as 'Our Love Is Here To Stay' is played softly over and* **Joan** *enters the spot looking exactly as she did twenty-five years ago. She puts her fingers to her lips.*

Joan   Shhhh, the room is dreaming . . .

Aylmer *gets up and they dance.*

Joan   Are you dead, Michael?

Aylmer   No, not yet.

Joan   Spirits, like angels, have trouble telling whether they're with the living or the dead. So we should adventure a prow in Galilee and shake with Jesus.

Aylmer   What does that mean?

Joan   Nothing, our business is to soar, so we must shun gravity. It's a message from another world, Michael.

Aylmer   What's it like on the other side?

Joan   I can't imagine. It has no dimension but I do have friends there – an American lady wrestler, a solicitor named Gerald Teckel, who left all his money to a musician who played the musical saw, and Balthazar Segal. But perhaps I knew them before I died, Michael, and I'm remembering them as you're remembering me.

Aylmer   Which I haven't done in years.

Joan   I didn't see the sunset last night but I heard about it. You've grown old well, Michael.

Aylmer   With money and success it's easy.

Joan   And Diana too. Still beautiful but she's always struck me as being so cold, every time she opens her mouth a light goes on . . . Are you happy, Michael?

Aylmer   No.

Joan   Then you should be. Who or what is served by all that expenditure of energy on suns, moons, planets, stars, comets and nebula, black holes and red dwarfs if men and women don't rejoice at the wonder of their existence?

Now I haven't got it I know its value. Which brings us to
Charlie.

Aylmer He took you from me.

Joan No, it was the bust of Bertie Russell – the man
who spent 300 pages proving one plus one equals two.
Was he thick? No, just slow and sex mad . . . A bust took
me from you. It could've been a Number 10 bus, a virus,
the prick from a rose's thorn. I plead for Charlie.

Aylmer Why?

Joan From the other side it isn't your disorder but your
order that looks so horrible. White-haired and slack-
jawed Charlie's feet are still as light as a four-year-old's.
He's terrible close-to but he turns and turns those who
can truly see his dancing. You called me back because of
Charlie. You wouldn't have thought of me so strongly if
he hadn't returned. It's all one, Michael . . . I must go.
Your memory of me is beginning to fade.

Aylmer Tell me of death and dying.

Joan Death is the other side of life which is turned away
from us. We can shed no light on it but our blood and
breath pass through both kingdoms so we should be at
home in both. There is neither here or hereafter but a
single unity which we share with the angels . . . (*She
laughs.*) . . . You said that, Michael, I didn't. Or rather
you made me say it.

Aylmer I did?

Joan It's what you wanted me to say so I said it.

Aylmer It's not true?

Joan It could be. I'm as much in the dark as you. I'm a
figment of your imagination, remember. All I know is I've
grown very fond of rats, they have such wonderful eyes
. . . Goodbye, Michael. Try not to lose yourself . . . and
think of me . . .

He attempts to kiss her but she slips out of his arms and into the darkness as the music stops and the spot fades out.

Scene Six

Lights up on Cardboard City. **Derelicts**, *amongst them* **Woods**, **Euston** *and* **Stoner**, *peer out of homes made of boxes and packing-cases and sing.*

All   'If you're spending your nights in a doss-house. / If you're spending your days in the streets. / And you're looking for work, and you find none / And you wish you had something to eat. / Remember it's your fault it happened. / There is something wrong with you / So you must take all the blame / And suffer the guilt and the shame. / For those in authority / Agree that your poverty / Is totally due / To you.'

A battered **Ketchum** *enters Stage Right to be met by* **Euston**, **Woods** *and* **Stoner**. *Other* **Derelicts** *look on.*

Euston   Did the Lituanians get you, Charlie? Last time we saw you you was unwired. Did they turn nasty after we left?

Ketchum   Nasty? Who Four-Eyes Aylmer? Never. Greeted me like a long lost . . . 'What's mine is yours' he says.

Stoner   So why are you here instead of there? We've got no decent loos for half a mile in each direction. Can't stand easy.

Ketchum   Had to leave. Matter of honour. I found out he'd nabbed my bird the moment my back was turned. Can you credit it? I didn't want to stay. Too disturbing for her with me around, realising just what she'd missed. Women used to take to me like ducks to green peas.

Euston   So you waved 'em goodbye forever and a day.

Ketchum Gave up, you mean? Never! I'll fight till my hair bleeds to get her back. She'll be mine. Just you watch!

Two derelicts, **Sebastian Vane** *who is tied together with string and* **Mrs Brown** *a bundle of old clothes with polythene bags on her feet and a tall head-dress of rags, enter.*

Vane My name's Sebastian Vane.

Ketchum Mine isn't.

Stoner Neither's mine come to think of it.

Woods Nor mine.

Vane Be that as it may. As official, self-appointed representatives of Cardboard City Community Association UK we've come on a delicate matter. These properties occupy an unrivalled position in the centre of London adjacent to one of the capital's premier landmarks. They lie in close proximity to various employment exchanges and soup kitchens and with easy access to the river and derelict building sites. They are desirable residences and we have a long waiting list.

Mrs Brown The fact is, Ketchum, the Association have voted to ask you to leave.

Vane Frankly we feel you lower the tone of the place and worse you'll bring down property values.

Ketchum You're moon-mad – got a touch of the rusty rifle. Everyone knows I'm all class.

Mrs Brown We have drunks, lunatics, murderers and misfits by the score but we can't have you. You make the air tremble as you pass!

Vane We're only tolerated here by the authorities so long as we don't cause trouble. We have to keep a low profile and creep softly.

Ketchum Creep? I've never crept 'cept into a woman's bed. In the old days beggers-on-the-fly like us were Freedom's Men and now look. Arse-crawlers to a man!

Mrs Brown You're a stirrer.

Vane And we don't want stirring. It's that potential that has us worried.

Ketchum Did you say potential? We'll agree on that. I'm white-haired and my teeth are falling but I've still got potential, buckets of the stuff. Open yer lugholes and listen to this bit of potential from England's finest.

Before anyone can stop him he puts the trumpet to his lips and blows. He hits a long piercing note of power and volume which reaches a crescendo and blows away every cardboard box and packing case to reveal, just before the fade out, astonished **Derelicts** *caught frozen like dummies in various domestic poses: washing in a tin bath, a family eating, a man reading, a woman cleaning, a couple making love.*

Darkness.

Scene Seven

Spot up on **Ketchum** *carrying his suitcase and battling against a great wind.*

Ketchum I should sue 'em. Let 'em face the combined might of Telford, Telford, Telford and Shankley. Where was Gunboat, Zac and Gaff when I got the boot? They said they were right behind me. Have you noticed the buggers are always right behind you, never up there with you when things turn narky? . . . I haven't time to go broody. But I've gotta box canny before I make my move. Watch and wait – then pounce! . . . (*He punches the wind and it immediately drops.*) I always win because I never think of Mondays!

Spot out.

Scene Eight

Lights up on a small private dining-room in an expensive restaurant. Doors Upstage Right and Left. Seated at a table Stage Centre are **Arthur Sidley, Diana, Mrs Aylmer** *who is very old and very deaf,* **Aylmer** *and* **Barnes**. *The* **Maître d'** *and a* **Waiter** *bustle about discreetly.* **Sidley** *taps a glass.*

Sidley I'd like to propose a toast to Michael and Diana – to you, Michael, on thirty years as a public figure on the eve of your knighthood, and you, Diana, on twenty-five years of marriage. I don't know which is harder.

Barnes You must be very proud of your son, Mrs Aylmer?

Mrs Aylmer Proud? Yes we Aylmers have always been proud. Even when we didn't have two half-pennies to rub together we never took in lodgers. Joan knows. Kindest daughter-in-law anyone could wish to have. And doesn't she stay young?

Diana No, Mother, I'm Diana, the other one . . . Was it wise to bring her out, Michael?

Aylmer She'll enjoy it . . . You're enjoying it aren't you, Mother?! But no toast, Arthur.

Diana That's right, this is just a quiet dinner with old friends. We thought it'd do us good. Michael's been a little low lately.

Sidley But surely a knighthood's what you always wanted, Michael? How can you be low?

Aylmer A touch of the talking blues. Thirty years of talking and writing words in the air, scratches in the sand – for who, for what?

Barnes The same feeling sometimes sweeps over me, that writing for the theatre is just an easy substitute for moral action.

Aylmer Explain yourself?

Barnes   When an audience weeps or laughs in the theatre, it feels it has done something virtuous merely by identifying with and experiencing the actions on stage. Noble feelings become a cheap substitute for noble actions. The public gives its tears and laughter to fictions and so thinks it's done enough. But real victims demand real attention. And that's a different story. Nobody's interested. The theatre's become an easy way out for everybody.

Diana   That has absolutely nothing to do with Michael being depressed!

Barnes   Well, I thought it was quite interesting.

Mrs Aylmer   I can tell you a story. The day before she died my friend, Mrs Harcourt – you remember Mrs Harcourt, Joan? She told her one-legged daughter not to worry, one day Prince Charming would come and sweep her off her foot. Anyway she took a taxi home that particular afternoon and the cabby hoped for a tip so he said, 'Have a nice day, Madam'. 'Listen,' said Mrs Harcourt, 'don't you poke your nose into my affairs. I'll have the kind of day I damn well want!'

Diana   Fascinating, Mother!

Mrs Aylmer   I thought you'd like it, Joan.

Aylmer   I think the problem is that looking back there's something missing and I don't know what it is.

Sidley   You sound a bit like a famous French singer. One evening a mob arrived in front of his hotel to give him an ovation for a performance. But he thought they'd come to lynch him because he'd been in such terrible voice that evening. In despair he jumped out of the hotel window and killed himself. Don't do it, Michael. As your publisher I can tell you it wouldn't be a good career move.

The **Others** *laugh.*

Mrs Aylmer   Did someone make a joke? Tell me a joke!

Sidley   Yes, well, coming here Mrs Aylmer, I saw an
elephant break a plate-glass shop window and suck up all
the jewellery on display and then gallop off. Some damn
policeman asked me if I could describe the elephant? I
said, 'No, of course not, it had a stocking over its face.'

As they laugh again a **Second Waiter** *appears, head down,
carefully carrying a pile of plates.*

Mrs Aylmer   I don't like elephants – it's their ears.

Sidley   Anyway, I'm determined to brighten the
atmosphere and make that toast. I'm raising my glass to
Michael and Diana Aylmer. It couldn't happen to nicer
people!

Sidley *and* **Barnes** *raise their glasses and drink as the*
Second Waiter *creeps up behind then, raises his head for
the first time and we see it is* **Ketchum***, dressed in an
absurdly ill-fitting waiter's jacket.*

As **Diana***,* **Sidley** *and* **Aylmer** *talk and* **Mrs Aylmer**
continues chewing breadsticks, **Ketchum** *puts an empty
plate in front of* **Barnes** *whilst never taking his eyes off*
Diana*.*

Barnes (*low*)   Waiter, this plate's got a crack in it.

Ketchum (*low*)   Eat – that's the steak. Listen, a word of
warning. They're serving wild rice. Don't be fooled. It's
really tame rice and they just stir it around in the kitchen
till it gets mad. Nobody knows the difference.

Mrs Aylmer (*low*)   Waiter, the soup smelt of kerosene.

Ketchum (*low*)   No, it smelt like it's supposed to smell –
of soap.

Ketchum *sidles round the table to behind* **Diana***. She does
not look up but continues talking with* **Sidley** *and* **Aylmer***.*

Diana   I'll have the fillet, no vegetables.

Ketchum   Vegetables is good for you, builds up your
strength. Di, it's me!

Diana *turns in horror.*

Aylmer   Not again!

Sidley   What's going on?

Barnes   It's him – Ketchum!

Ketchum   I'm in disguise. Brilliant, isn't it?! Even my beard's fake. The real one's in my pocket.

Diana   It's your fault, Michael, you should've prosecuted him.

Ketchum   What?! Is this the thanks I get for dressing up like a poncy penguin?!

He tears off his shirt-front and exits Stage Left.

Sidley   I don't understand.

Mrs Aylmer   Who was that man, Michael?

Aylmer   The one who killed Joan.

Mrs Aylmer   Killed Joan? You're going a bit mental, son. Joan's not dead. You're not dead are you, dear?

Diana   I'm not Joan!

Barnes   I thought I recognised him. If you're a writer you have to be pretty sharp at spotting people.

Sidley   I'm not privy to the plot. Will somebody please fill me in?

Diana   There's no time.

Aylmer   Call the management.

Barnes   Where's the Maître d'?!

Ketchum *strides in Stage Left this time, dressed in the* **Maître d**'s *jacket.*

Ketchum   Quiet please! This is a respectable restaurant – four star and oak-leaf cluster.

Sidley   It's him again!

Ketchum *rips his trousers as he clumsily pulls out an old gun from his pocket. The others 'freeze'.*

Ketchum You're not dealing with an idiot. I came prepared.

As a **Waiter** *enters Stage Left with a tray of food* **Ketchum** *gestures with the gun and the barrel drops off. As the others rush forward,* **Ketchum** *whips out another gun from his other pocket.*

Sidley Is he mad?

Ketchum Not me. Maybe Smarty-Pants over there who thinks he deserves a knighthood for yakking – I know England's gone to the dogs, but it hasn't sunk that low. And his ma, who swears her daughter-in-law isn't dead. 'Course she is. If anyone should know I should. Then there's that loony calling himself Barnes who thinks he's a writer. And you've got bloody mad eyes. Any chance of you publishing my autobiography? 'A Life on the Open Road' by C. Ketchum, Bart?

Mrs Aylmer Where's the food?! The service in this restaurant is terrible.

Ketchum Di, I've put my head into a moose for you so just pin back your lugholes and listen. Where will you find another love like mine? I'm about as musical as a pig with its nose caught under a gate but you've made me a poet, Di. (*Singing.*) 'He remembered me from long ago, / When we were young he said. I know your name, your name is Jill. / I told him it was Fred. / Oh why can't they remember the tender little things? / Like one glass eye. / A broken nose. / And a simple name like Fred.' That says it all. Don't be content with second best. I'm the real thing!

Barnes Somebody make a Citizen's Arrest.

Sidley How do you do that?

Aylmer We've got to rush him.

Ketchum   Stay back! I once played tennis with the man who killed Rasputin and I never took my eye off the ball.

He points the gun at the ceiling above them and pulls the trigger. It clicks but does not fire. **Ketchum** *throws the weapon away irritably and as the others surge forward he produces a third gun from his crotch. The others hesitate.*

Barnes   It's probably as wonky as the others.

Ketchum   Could be . . .

He points the gun at the floor and pulls the trigger. This time the gun fires. All, including **Ketchum**, *jump back in fright.* **Mrs Aylmer** *gestures angrily.*

Mrs Aylmer   This is too much! Waiter, I'm sitting here starving.

Ketchum   And I'm standing here with a song in my heart and a gun in my hand. So what's it to be, Di? Him or me, yes or no?

Diana   No, no, no, no, no, no, no. NO!

Ketchum   You've got a problem, Di.

Diana   Yes, it's called good taste.

Ketchum   If that's your attitude I've got nothing more to say.

Diana   You've got nothing more to say, I don't believe it.

Ketchum   Well, come to think of it I . . .

Diana   You're everything I hate and fear, Ketchum. You're everything *hairy*!

Ketchum   I don't believe it.

Diana   I'm a Safety-Firster, first, last and always.

Ketchum (*gasping*)   Di . . . the heart . . . the heart . . .

Diana   Don't talk about my heart. The heart is a muscle that pumps blood not love. And it's never pumped for you!

Ketchum Not your heart . . . mine . . . feel fingers . . . squeezing . . . (*He collapses onto his knees.*) Death is squeezing . . . Di, hear my last words . . . Don't give the dog any more coffee!

He pitches forward flat on his face and lies still. The others fearfully creep forward and gather round him in a semicircle.

Diana He's faking again.

Aylmer No, it's real.

Still seated **Mrs Aylmer** *impatiently bangs the table with her spoon.*

Mrs Aylmer Let's eat! Let's eat! Let's eat!

Lights out.

Scene Nine

Sound of heartbeat in the darkness. Choir sings 'Poor Old Joe' in hushed tones.

Lights up on hospital ward. **Ketchum** *in bed Stage Centre. White screens. The beds on either side of him are empty.* **Nurse Dudley** *is checking his medical chart.*

Ketchum I've got a complaint, Florence. Somebody washed me when I wasn't looking.

Nurse Dudley That was me. Regulation – you were filthy.

Ketchum But you soaked me in water!

Dr Ford *enters Stage Right.*

Dr Ford I wouldn't complain if I were you. You're lucky to be alive.

Ketchum I know you. When I told you I was a kleptomaniac you said, 'Take these pills. And remember if they don't work I'm in the market for a video.'

Nurse Dudley Did you say that, Doctor?

Dr Ford   Of course not.

Ketchum   Would I spread a story like that if it wasn't true?!

Nurse Dudley   Calm yourself, Mr Ketchum. You just suffered a severe heart attack and you must stay quiet. We'd put you under sedation but it doesn't seem to work.

Ketchum *immediately falls back on the bed.*

Ketchum   They'll stop at nothing. I'm an old soldier who served England well.

Dr Ford   We've checked and there's no record of you ever being a soldier. In fact there's no record of you at all before your trial, no birth certificate, nothing.

Ketchum   Perhaps I wasn't born then? Did you get messages out to all and sundry, Nurse Nightingale?

Nurse Dudley   Yes, though I don't know why I should bother.

Euston, Woods and **Stoner** *enter tentatively Stage Left.*

Stoner   Squad reporting for duty, sir.

Nurse Dudley   Gentlemen, you may stay for a short time but don't excite Mr Ketchum.

Ketchum   You heard what Florence said, don't excite me. Don't talk dirty.

Nurse Dudley and **Dr Ford** *exit Stage Left.*

Ketchum   Why do you sidle into the room like that as if you were apologising? Come in bold. What've you brought? Where's the gifts – the flowers, the chocs, the hothouse peaches and such?

Euston   I brought you some cherries. But we ate 'em. (*Offers a bag.*) Don't know if you can do anything with the stones?

Stoner   You could plant them if you had a pot. Lovely place this, Charlie. You've landed lucky again, the walls are solid and the toilets are beautiful.

Ketchum I'm on my last legs, dying by inches and you don't even bring me a seedless grape. There's gratitude, there's friendship!

Woods We're not friends of yours, Charlie, we just happen to know you but, sure, we've brought you some plain jake.

He takes out two bottles from a carrier-bag and hands one to **Ketchum**. *They all start drinking from the bottles.*

Ketchum All's forgiven and forgotten . . . Truth is, I'm feeling like a trumped Charlie, everything ruined by Chinese cheap labour. It's hard breathing now when I always breathed easy. Give us a song to lighten the heart. But keep it low, lads.

Stoner What'll it be? 'Reveille' or better yet, 'The Last Post'?

Ketchum No, a little close harmony on my current favourite. Can't get enough of it. 'My Name Is Fred' if you please.

As **Euston, Woods** *and* **Stoner** *come together to form a barber-shop quartet,* **Ketchum** *picks up the metal bedpan. He strikes it with the bottle to get the note for the singers.*

Euston ⎫
Woods ⎬ *(singing softly)* 'He remembered me from
Stoner ⎭ long ago. / When we were both young, he said. / I know your name, your name is Jill. / I told him it was Fred.'

Ketchum *(singing softly)* 'That's what I said. / My name is Fred. / Not George or even Bill. / Try to recall. / It's not Jill at all. / It's always, but always has been Fred.'

All *(singing softly)* 'Oh why can't they remember the tender little things? / Like one glass eye. / A broken nose. / And a simple name like Fred.'

As **Ketchum** *flops back onto the bed and closes his eyes,* **Dr Ford** *enters Stage Right with* **Diana** *and* **Aylmer**. **Woods** *and* **Euston** *quickly hide the bottles.*

Dr Ford He's a miracle. He had a massive heart attack which would've killed any normal man. But he survived.

Aylmer He begged us to visit him. Do you know why?

Diana I'd just like to know why you've come, Michael? It's obviously another trick.

Aylmer I don't think so. Anyway there's no need for *you* to be here if you don't want to be.

Diana You can't be trusted alone with him.

Barnes *sidles on behind them.*

Barnes Of course this really isn't my scene but I couldn't resist it. I'll hover on the edges.

They arrive at **Ketchum's** *bed.* **Euston, Woods** *and* **Stoner** *shuffle awkwardly.*

Euston He seems to've gone to sleep, Doc, just like that.

Dr Ford Yes, they often drop off unexpectedly and then they suddenly wake up again, until one day they suddenly don't.

He exits Stage Right. They stand around the bed in silence.

Aylmer Charlie . . . Charlie . . . Charlie . . . Come on Charlie.

Ketchum *sits up.*

Ketchum Piss off!

Diana You see.

Ketchum It's what I said when you woke me up before. Piss off . . . after that it was downhill all the way. You couldn't let sleeping old dogs lie, Mike lad . . . Ooh I feel poorly. Plain jake isn't what it was.

Euston The Lituanians get us all in the end.

Ketchum That's why I asked you here, friends. To hear my last words. 'Cept I don't know any. You must have boned up on a few, what-ever-you-call-yourself?

Barnes Last words? 'Die, my dear doctor? That's the last thing I shall do' are good lastwords . . . 'Now what?!' is even better.

Ketchum I'll need 'em soon enough.

Diana He's lying.

Aylmer How do you know he's lying?

Diana His lips're moving. He'll never die! We'll never be rid of him!

Ketchum Sometimes you've got a tongue like a chainsaw, Di. It's something you should watch. When you're like this you remind me a bit of Nurse Gladys Beavis – you remember, lads.

Woods Sure, she was the only woman I've known who could kick-start a Boeing jet.

Ketchum That's the one. But forgive and forget. I asked you here to hear the last will and testament of yours truly. I'm leaving it all to you, Di.

Diana I don't want you to leave me anything.

Ketchum I haven't got anything. But it's still all yours . . . No, plain jake isn't what it was . . . used to perk me up now it makes me peaky . . . (*Gasping.*) My heart's doing funny things . . .

Barnes Should we call the doctor?

Diana He's faking it.

Ketchum No . . . I want a quiet going if I'm going with the fighting and the fun's all down the toilet.

Stoner That's where everything ends up.

Ketchum I'd like my death to be a bit traditional . . . gather round and sing the old songs . . .

As they gather round his bed, bow their heads and hum the negro spiritual 'Deep River' a **Figure** *enters through the wall behind* **Ketchum** *dressed in black robes, a cowl and carrying a scythe. Only* **Ketchum** *sees him.*

Ketchum   Who're you?

Death (*wearily*)   Who do you think I am dressed like this? I'm Death. Your Death.

Ketchum *grabs the metal bedpan and smashes* **Death** *over the head with it.* **Death** *slumps to the floor and rolls under the bed.*

Ketchum   Bloody well wait, short-arse! I'm not ready yet.

The **Others** *look up.*

Aylmer   What did you say?

Ketchum   I said I'm not ready yet.

Diana   You see, you see! I knew he wouldn't be.

Ketchum   I've changed my mind. Let's break open a bottle.

He and **Woods** *produce their bottles and drink.*

Aylmer   Are you supposed to do that? Where's the doctor?

Ketchum   In Harley Street by now, coining the old masula – them and their hypocrites oath. Don't worry the old ticker's working full pelt again . . . We'll have a party. If you're sorry about waking me up when I was young and so handsome ordinary things just stopped and looked at me, I'm sorry about bashing Joany with Bertie.

Joan *enters through the wall behind him.*

Joan   It's all one now, Charlie.

Ketchum   You've got a good heart, Joan lass.

Aylmer   Yes she has. She made me come here to see you, Charlie.

Diana   Who're you talking to? Am I included in this? No, of course not. I'm never included in anything. Why is getting what you want from life so disappointing?

Ketchum *takes his trumpet from under his pillow and stands up on the bed.*

Ketchum　I've got the devil in me breeches again and an itch to play the old tunes. Zac, strike up the spoons.

Woods　Sure, what'll it be, Charlie?

Ketchum　'Rolling Round The World', what else?

As he clambers off the bed he hits **Death**, *who is sliding out from under, with his trumpet and starts playing raucously with* **Euston**, **Woods** *and* **Stoner**.

Aylmer　Charlie!

Ketchum　Everybody join in.

Barnes　I can't hold a tune.

Ketchum　Don't hold it, sing it! You too, Di.

With **Ketchum** *leading they sing raggedly.*

All (*singing*)　'Rolling round the world, looking for the sunshine. / That never seems to come our way. / Rolling round the world where every little milestone / Seems to look at us and say / Goodbye rainy days, goodbye snow. / Got no use for you, got to go . . .'

Dr Ford *and* **Nurse Dudley** *rush in Stage Right.*

Dr Ford　What's going on?!

Ketchum　I'm feeling young again. You all look lovely. (*He kisses* **Nurse Dudley**.) One for you . . . (*He kisses* **Diana**.) One for sweet Di . . . (*He blows* **Joan** *a kiss*.) And one for Joan wherever you are . . . Right one more chorus. We'll pick it up from 'Goodbye rainy days . . .'

Euston, Woods *and* **Stoner** *start playing whilst* **Ketchum** *continues singing 'Goodbye rainy days, goodbye snow . . .'*

All (*singing*)　'Got no use for you! Gotta go! / Rolling round the world looking for the sunshine. / We know we're going to find some day . . .'

Ketchum   *Ahhhh*!

Ketchum *lets out a cry of pain, drops his trumpet and clutches himself.*

Dr Ford   I knew it! His heart!

Ketchum   No . . . bowels . . . like the song says I've got to go! . . . Quick!

Nurse Dudley   The bedpan! Where's the bedpan?

The others frantically search for the bedpan as **Ketchum** *struggles to pull down his pyjamas.*

Diana   It's disgusting.

Ketchum   No. It's life.

In the confusion **Nurse Dudley** *finds the bedpan, rushes forward, stumbles over a drunken* **Stoner** *and cannons straight into* **Ketchum** *just as he starts to bend over. The bedpan jams right into* **Ketchum**'s *backside.*

Ketchum   Ahh . . . Get it off! . . . It's stuck! . . .

Barnes   It's what?

Ketchum   You deaf as well as stupid? It's stuck!

He wriggles his backside. The bedpan remains jammed on. The others stare and start laughing despite themselves, at the sight of **Ketchum** *with a bedpan stuck to his bottom, wriggling furiously.*

Diana *starts laughing. It is the first time we have ever seen her laugh.*

Diana   Poor Charlie . . .

Ketchum   Don't laugh, you buggers. I've got to go . . .

Death's *scythe sneaks out from under the bed and hooks him back.* **Ketchum** *stares at the blade of the scythe round his waist forcing him to sit on the edge of the bed, still stuck to the bedpan.*

Ketchum   Oh dear . . . I'm going all right . . . oh dear . . . oh dear . . . (*The others stop laughing.*) I'm going –

both ways fore and aft . . . going with the light . . . life going and the light going . . . (**Joan** *sits beside him.*) Oh dear . . . oh dear . . . Last words. I was given some last words but I can't remember 'em. No time left . . . Farty Death has me in his grip . . . all the things I could've done and didn't do . . . didn't do . . . (**Joan** *takes his hand.*) I thought I'd go with choirs and such and some ponce recalling all the good things I've done and me blowing my trumpet. Doesn't matter I suppose, going's going . . . Still I didn't expect to go like this, with me pants down, a bleeding bedpan stuck on me arse and not able to think of one bloody last word . . . Shit!

He topples slowly forward off the edge of the bed, ending with his face on the floor and his bare bottom high in the air still crowned with the bedpan.

*As **Dr Ford** examines him the lights begin to fade out.*

Dr Ford   He's dead.

Euston
Woods } Poor old Charlie.
Stoner

Euston   Sure, he won't rest in peace.

Stoner   Never did.

Woods   The Lits can't get him now.

Aylmer   He must be dead. It's so quiet. Out there in space there's an exploding super-Nova to tell us that Charlie's really gone. Here, even the air is still.

Diana   He hasn't gone. He'll never go. He's faking again!

Barnes   Not this time. It's the end.

*The 'Funeral March' is played raggedly by **Ketchum**'s band in the darkness.*

Epilogue

The 'Funeral March' dies away.

Lights up to show a high tech office. The side wall is made up of rows of computer screens all showing various images of spectacular disasters without sound. There is a desk opposite Stage Right. On the wall behind it a map of the city. Upstage Centre a small lift with an iron gate. Door Stage Left.

Mr Nicolaus, *a dark-suited bureaucrat sits writing at the desk, as someone knocks tentatively at the door.*

Nicolaus   Come!

The door opens hesitantly and **Ketchum** *enters dressed in his old coat and carrying his trumpet.* **Nicolaus** *motions him to the chair in front of his desk.*

Nicolaus   Please sit down . . . (*Consulting the file.*) Mr Ketchum.

Ketchum   'Ere, 'ere, what's going on then? Who're you?

Nicolaus *has been reading the file.*

Nicolaus   I'm sorry. What did you say?

Ketchum   What's your name?

Nicolaus   Nicolaus. Mr Nicolaus. Of course I've had many names over the years: The Zoroasters called me Ahriman; the Babylonians, Lady Nina and the Christians, Lucifer, due to a misreading of Isaiah 14:12. I've had nicknames too, the 'Old Gentleman', the 'Ugly One', the 'Angel of Edom', but on the whole they don't amuse me although I confess 'Auld Hornie' has a certain charm. I'm also known as The Tempter, The Destroyer, The Fallen Angel, Prince of Darkness, Demon of Demons, The Evil One, Satan. Actually I prefer the Great Administrator.

Ketchum   Jesus Christ, it's Old Nick hisself.

Nicolaus   'Sir', to you.

Ketchum   If you're Old Nick, what am I?

Nicolaus   Dead.

Ketchum   *Ahhhh!*

Nicolaus (*looking at watch*)   You died exactly two seconds ago. You've made excellent time.

Ketchum   No, Charlie's being jossed solid. If you're Old Nick where's yer little horns and prongs then?

Nicolaus   Horns and prongs are passé. Gone with the fire and brimstone. Down here we move with the times. Upstairs, of course, they never change. Paradise is the same now, as it was then. But Hell is very much in the modern style. After all, this is the blueprint for Hell on earth.

Ketchum   I can see and hear and smell. I ain't dead! Charlie's alive-o!

Nicolaus *opens a drawer, takes out a revolver, points it straight at* **Ketchum** *and fires.* **Ketchum** *is sent careering backwards over the chair.* **Nicolaus** *puts the revolver away as* **Ketchum** *lies moaning on the carpet.*

Nicolaus   You'll find the bullet on the floor beside you. You can't be killed because you're already dead and in the portals of Hell. Now, I'm extremely busy.

Ketchum *crawls back onto the chair.*

Ketchum   But I can't be in Hell, Mr Nick. I'm British.

Nicolaus   We'll try not to hold that against you. But remember, you're not actually in Hell yet, only the portals. That's what this interview's for. According to our records you do have one murder to your credit, though unfortunately, it was to all intents and purposes, an accident. However, accident or not, it was a step in the right direction; it showed willing. I like that. So, you'll be pleased to know, Mr Ketchum, you can go to Hell. Let me put you in the picture. (*He points to the wall map behind him.*) This is a small section of what is laughingly called the 'Dark Regions'.

Ketchum   Must be big.

Nicolaus   No, it's so small you can't see it with the naked eye, so minute it could fit into a single atom. I don't wish to oversell the Bottomless Pit, but I'm certain we offer something you'll find nowhere else – a feeling of contentment. We give our souls security and an eternal peace in exchange for a worthless freedom.

Ketchum   It sounds like Hell.

Nicolaus   It *is* Hell.

Ketchum   Piss me!

Nicolaus   That's another thing. Curb your language. There's no place in the Abyss for such gross manifestations of individuality. And that smell of yours. It's too much like the odour of sanctity for comfort. You'll have to wash regularly. My favourites are invariably clean, abstemious, mildly spoken . . .

As the phone rings and he picks it up, **Ketchum** *blows a piercing trumpet blast in his ear.* **Nicolaus** *leaps up in surprise and* **Ketchum** *hits him over the head with his trumpet.*

Ketchum   Bloody Old Nick, that's one for your knob!

He clambers up on the desk and starts unzipping his flies.

Nicolaus   What're you doing?

Ketchum   Getting out Uncle Wiggly. I'm going to piss on the Devil from a great height. Watch out, here comes the One-Eyed Wonder!

At that moment **Two Attendants** *rush on Stage Left.*

Nicolaus   Get rid of him!

They haul **Ketchum** *off the desk, still vainly trying to unzip his flies.*

Ketchum Wait, wait, I'm letting loose Little Percy!

Attendants Up, sir?

Nicolaus Up!

They bundle **Ketchum** *into the lift Upstage.*

Ketchum Short-arsed squirt! This is Charlie K you're dealing with now!

Nicolaus Foul-mouthed lout! Good riddance. And stay up!

He presses the lift button. All lights dim out except the one in the lift.

As **Ketchum** *goes silent, his coat mysteriously falls from his shoulders. Underneath he is found to be wearing long combinations of dazzling white.*

A soft rhythmic clapping is heard, as the lift starts its slow journey up. The clapping grows louder as **Angels** *with tiny wings and halos and dressed in white night-shirts appear in a spot in the Flies Upstage Right.*

Angels (*singing*) 'Nine o'clock and nothing doin'. / What a dull and dreary night!? Just a good time gone to ruin, / Not a bit o' fun in sight. / Take a look what just blew in. / Hurry up, unlock the door. / It's that great big muggins Charlie Ketchum / We've been waiting for . . . Clap hands! Here comes Charlie! / Clap hands, good old Charlie. / Clap hands, here comes Charlie now! / Clap hands, join the party. / Clap hands, meet old Charlie. / Clap hands, Charlie take a bow! / We'll have drinks with Charlie at our table. / Grab a chair, move over there, / and let him sit with Gabriel. / Clap hands, here comes Charlie. / Clap hands, good old Charlie. / Clap hands, here comes Charlie now!'

In the slow moving lift **Ketchum** *puts his gleaming trumpet to his lips and blows a wobbly 'Tan-tivey, Tan-tivey!' A*

slight pause, and away in the darkness Gabriel's horn
answers, 'Tan-tivey, Tan-tivey!'

Ketchum *looks up as he ascends into the darkness to meet*
his Maker.

Heaven's Blessings

Characters

Tobit
Anna
Ahikar
Tobias
Kanach
Raphael
First Shape
Second Shape
Third Shape
Raguel
Sarah
Rabbi Baanah
Asmodeus
God's voice

Prologue

Spot up Downstage Centre on **Tobit** *in front of a huge wall, finishing covering a grave by the light of a solitary lamp.*

Tobit Why am I burying a dead Jew outside the walls of Nineveh in the dead of night when I could be home drinking wine out of warm bowls? The law says dead Jews must be left unburied. It's a terrible thing. The first Adam was made of earth and it's natural to return to it. There's a bond between the soul and the body even after death and the spirit of the unburied wander this lost world crying for repose. My wife says we are only exiles in Assyria and should live invisible . . . Holy Lord God of Israel, hear thy servant Tobit, son of Tobeil, who used to live in Thisbe in Upper Galilee, above Hazor . . . south of Kedash . . . just north of Shephat. Yes, that Tobit . . . Though there must be thousands of Tobits in the world you should remember me, I stayed faithful when the rest of Thisbe forsook Thee and returned to worshipping the golden calves of Jeroboam. I obey the law of Moses and you, Lord, who created Adam, hollowed out his bones, formed his marrow and his heart, and whose world is a world of splendour. My wife complains we live poor because of you, Lord. I tell her it could be worse. Our rings may have fallen off but we still have our fingers. Ahikar, King Esarhaddon's Chief Minister, still helps us. Well, why shouldn't he? He *is* my nephew. Another apostate and backslider, Lord, and my son Tobias is none too strong for you, either. Why do sons always want to disappoint their fathers? If you have one, Lord, you'll discover they never go the right way . . . (*There is a sound in the darkness.*) Who's out there? . . . I'm just planting some corn . . . It's the best time . . . Under a full moon . . . Is anyone there? . . . No . . . Good . . . (*He pats down the grave.*) May your bones lie soft, brother, and the earth light upon you . . . (*He picks up the lantern and moves off Stage Left.*) Why am I burying a dead Jew outside the

walls of Nineveh in the dead of night? Because I believe
. . . But that's no answer . . .

Scene One

Lights up on a small barely furnished room in **Tobit**'s *house.
There is a brass candelabra on the wooden table Stage Right,
which is set for dinner. The front door is Upstage Centre, a
cupboard door Upstage Left and the exit to the kitchen, Stage
Left.* **Anna**, **Tobit**'s *wife, helps* **Ahikar** *off with his cloak.*

Anna   He's dug more holes than a troop of midnight
moles. He's sliding another dead one under now.

Ahikar   Anyone you know?

Anna   No, all the dead are strangers. He does it all for
free.

Ahikar   Free or not, it's still against the law.
Disobedience is death. Esarhaddon is strong on
disobedience even more than his father – Esarhaddon is
less secure. So when he takes hot baths everyone sweats.
Ever since his army was beaten by Syria and Judah he's
made it hard for Jews in Nineveh. He can't forgive his
enemies even when they're dead. In his eyes, their deaths
only deepen their crimes. By defying him, Uncle Tobit
puts us all in danger.

Anna   I've told him but he only listens to God.

Ahikar   And it's the wrong one. In Galilee we
worshipped the God of Israel, obeyed the law of Moses.
In Nineveh we should worship the gods of the Assyrians –
Assur, Adad or even Nergal – and obey the law of King
Esarhaddon. I can't protect you forever, Aunt.

Anna   You're a good boy, Zacharia.

Ahikar   Don't call me Zacharia, it's Ahikar, Lord
Ahikar . . . How many is he burying out there? Don't
answer. If he doesn't come soon, I'll have to go.

Anna But it's Pentecost. I've cooked your favourite, Quom bread.

Ahikar Quom bread? At Court we dine on truffles and figs, geese in ghee, and apricots in date syrup but I still long for the taste of Quom bread and spring water from Lebanon.

Anna Our land was rich and fruitful then and far away we could see the white hills of Gelboa.

Ahikar Space without corners and the eastern slopes were all golden down to the River Jordan.

Tobit *hurries in Upstage Centre, quickly closing the door behind him and putting down his shovel and lantern.*

Tobit (*low*) Shhh, the night has ears and noses too. I think perhaps someone was following me.

Ahikar I must go! My position demands it.

Tobit No . . . I was mistaken. A drink, Nephew. I have a fresh batch of Hebron wine.

Anna Which he hasn't had time to sell. Too busy digging holes.

Tobit *pours wine from a jug into bowls.*

Tobit Your health, Zacharia.

Anna Don't call him Zacharia. You'll need to wash before you eat after all that night farming . . . Speak to him, Zacharia.

She exits into the kitchen, Stage Left.

Ahikar Uncle, look how you're fallen. Once you had the old King Shalmaneser's favour. He made you his Purveyor but you had to anger his successor by burying dead Jews. Now you have nothing – and very little of that.

Tobit The Lord will provide.

Anna (*poking her head back in*) He hasn't provided much of late! I know He can't help with money but at least He could give us a sympathetic groan.

Tobit I used to feel sorry for myself because I had no shoes until I met old Shindel who had no feet.

Ahikar Remember the sound maxim: 'If you can't win, give in.'

Tobit Remember the better one: 'If you can't win, you must win.'

Ahikar Obey the law, Uncle.

Tobit But I perform a public service, Nephew. Corpses become the meal of flies, greedy for human flesh and as bodies rot, diseases spread.

Ahikar Disobedience is a disease more deadly than rotting corpses. To transgress the law, twist it to one's own purpose is a sin against all authority, even the gods. There is no greater crime. States are devoured by it, for with disobedience anarchy smothers all and our world is drowned in blood. Only obey your ruler.

Tobit I obey the God of Abraham who rules my heart.

Ahikar His rule is over. The elders of our tribe kicked Him out long before we Jews were exiled to Nineveh. Every year we journeyed to Jerusalem to pray at the temple and pay our tithes to fat priests who sniggered behind their beards at thick Galilean yokels. We naturally decided if the priests despised us it was likely their God did too. And so we forswore Him. I've often wondered why you remained faithful, Uncle?

Tobit For the believer there is no question, for the non-believer no answer. Remaining faithful was a matter of faith.

Anna *comes back with a bowl of water and a towel which she places on the table.* **Tobit** *washes his hands.*

Anna We serve Him beyond all reason.

Tobit   Because He is beyond all reason.

Ahikar   I'll give you a drachma if you tell me where your God lives.

Tobit   I'll give you two if you tell me where He doesn't.

He sits and **Anna** *kneels and washes his feet.*

Ahikar   Most gods are much alike. Look on the Assyrian, Assur. He's a war god too. They pray to him like all men pray to their god. 'Oh mighty Assur, help us tear our enemies to pieces, cut down their women and children, lay waste their lands. Because we adore you, Lord, blight their lives and stain the desert with their blood.' Sometimes he answers, sometimes he doesn't. He's as fickle as all the rest.

Tobit   The God of Israel is a God of love but we don't see it for we are not open to Him and so we cry only for blood.

Ahikar   When I first came to Court I went to the royal menagerie and I saw a lion and a lamb in the same cage. Wonderful I thought, the dream of Israel is realised. I congratulated the Royal Keeper. 'Tell me, friend,' I asked, 'how do you fly in the face of earthly convention and make the lion lie down with the lamb?' 'Easy,' he said, 'every morning I put another lamb in the cage . . .' A killing wind blows, Uncle, tack before it as sailors do in a storm, else we all drown.

Anna   The dead have no friends, so let the dead bury the dead.

She finishes washing **Tobit**'s *feet and gets up.*

Ahikar   The king's rage will pass. He'll win a small victory on some distant frontier and feel magnanimous. Or the carrion-stink of a thousand corpses will finally reach royal nostrils and he'll let the law fall into disuse. Meanwhile, do not break it, I beg: think of your family.

Anna   If we die, who'll serve Israel?

Tobit Yes, it's true, who'll serve? . . . For Israel's sake and yours, wife, I'll suspend night-digging.

The door Upstage Centre bursts open and **Tobit***'s son,* **Tobias** *rushes in.*

Tobias Father, did you hear it? A fight across the street. Old Azarial from Shephat and Simeon of Gilead.

Anna Those two old fools are always fighting. It keeps them alive.

Tobias Not any more. Azarial was telling the story of the holy goat who roams the roads of time waiting for midnight when he touches the stars with his horns to make them sing the glory of Creation. 'It's a miracle,' says Azarial. 'Anyone who believes in miracles is an idiot,' says Simeon. 'Anyone who doesn't is a non-believer,' says Azarial. As they start fighting, Azarial thumps Simeon in the chest and the old man keels over gasping, 'I see the goat . . .' and dies.

Anna Dies? Like dead?

Tobias Dead, dead.

Tobit Dead?

He moves compulsively to the door, Upstage Centre.

Ahikar Uncle?

Anna Tobey?

Tobias Father!

Before anyone can stop him, **Tobit** *grabs his lantern and rushes out Upstage Centre, slamming the door behind him.*

Anna The Lord has him by the throat, knees and nostrils. It's a sickness.

Ahikar My cloak! I've stayed too long.

Anna It's your fault, Tobias. One whiff of a dead Jew and the digging's on him.

Tobias Not this time. See, he's left his shovel.

He picks up **Tobit**'s *shovel.*

Anna   Then he's just gone to see if old Simeon is truly dead or not. Pour Zach more wine.

She takes the bowl and towel back into the kitchen Stage Left, whilst **Tobias** *pours* **Ahikar** *another bowl of wine.*

Ahikar   There's no crime in looking at dead Jews. At least not yet.

Tobias   He may not be burying old Simeon but he'll be burying others soon enough leaving me to take care of the business. These are my tax-free years and I want to enjoy them instead of working myself to death. Ahikar, can't you stop him?

Ahikar   I've tried. Your mother will tell you, I've tried.

Anna *returns.*

Anna   He's tried, son. He's tried.

Tobias   Well, if you've tried . . .

Ahikar   But he won't listen. He's as stiff-necked as the God he worships. That's one of the qualities I find distasteful about the God of Israel. He always has to be right, numero uno, no other god but Him.

Tobias   He won't change.

Ahikar   Neither will your father. Everyone else does. If I thought I am now, what I was then, I wouldn't want to live.

Anna   Tobit's too old, too proud, too touched by glory and doesn't see the rest of us are not made of hero stuff. All we want is to live in the ease of life.

The door Upstage Centre suddenly opens and **Tobit** *half falls in carrying a body.*

Ahikar   What is it?

Tobit   Old Simeon.

Ahikar   Why did I ask?

Anna Is he dead?

Tobit All over.

Tobias (*shutting the door*) Why is it people like old Simeon find time to die?

Anna But what's he doing dead in our house?

Tobias *helps put the dead body in a chair.*

Tobit I couldn't leave him, cold eyes staring up at the stars. He can rest here till it's clear to plant him under.

Ahikar Quom bread or no Quom bread, I'm leaving!

Tobit I'd wait, Nephew. I saw some Imperial Guards searching out there in the dark.

Ahikar Imperial Guards?

There is loud knocking on the door Upstage Centre.

Tobit That's them.

He crosses to open the door. **Ahikar** *and* **Tobias** *haul him back.*

Ahikar Quick, hide the body.

Tobias The cupboard!

He and **Ahikar** *grab the corpse and rush across the room with it. As* **Anna** *opens the cupboard door for them Upstage Left, another corpse falls out, stiff as a board. They jump back in fright.*

Anna Tobey!

Tobit Forgive me, my dear, I quite forgot I'd stacked him ready for planting later.

There is more loud knocking.

Anna (*calling*) Yes, who is it?

Kanach's voice Captain Kanach . . . Imperial Guards . . . Open!

As the knocking continues, **Ahikar** *and* **Tobias** *rush
Simeon's corpse back into the chair, whilst* **Anna** *and* **Tobit**
push the second body back into the cupboard. **Tobias, Anna**
and **Ahikar** *then dive into chairs round the table with the
corpse a split second before* **Tobit** *opens the door Upstage
Centre and* **Captain Kanach** *enters.*

Kanach   Were you all asleep?

Anna   No, fearful, Captain. Robbers infest Nineveh at
night. And the army provides no protection.

Kanach   We've more important matters, woman.
Traitors, spies, enemies of the Empire are within the
gates.

Ahikar   Captain, I am the Lord Ahikar, Keeper of the
Signet, Administrator and Treasurer to King
Esarhaddon. And I'm dining here with my friends,
Brother Tobit, his wife and son.

Kanach *immediately snaps to attention and steps straight
on the shovel which springs up and hits him in the face. He
does not react other than spitting out two teeth.*

Kanach   My Lord Ahikar. I recognise you from Court,
Sire. I used to be Second Guard of the Fifth Gate before I
was promoted. We had a report that two Jews were
fighting near here and one was left for dead, though we
can't find any sign of the body. Did you hear anything?

The others shake their heads including the dead Simeon:
Tobias *is manipulating him from behind his chair.*

Ahikar   No one heard a sound.

Kanach   If there is a dead one, we're here to see he's not
buried. It's against the law.

Ahikar   What do you think of that, Captain? – leaving
corpses unburied.

Kanach   I've seen the dead piled high as mountains on a
hundred forgotten battlefields, so it's not new to me. But
I confess, I've always given my own men soft restings

underground where I could. And I'd hope they'd do the same for me. When my first wife died, they asked if she should be cremated, embalmed or just buried. 'All three,' I told them, 'why take chances?' I understand the need for burial, but if I found any Jews doing it, I'd cut 'em down.

Anna You'd feel no compunction?

Kanach Does any man feel compunction following his trade? I must join my men.

He starts to go.

Tobit A bowl of wine before you leave, Captain?

The others look at him in fury but it is too late.

Kanach That's good of you, Master Tobit. (**Tobit** *pours him some wine.*) A toast – the Empire, the King and the gods. (*He drinks.*) Good wine . . . I've nothing against dead Jews except my orders. In fact, their God Abraham or whatever his name is, is much to my taste. A god who tramples His enemies underfoot, dashes their brains against rocks, is for me. In battle it helps to know there's a killer god on your side. I know, I've fought from Nubia to Elam, from Thebes to the kingdom of Van. I've seen all my brothers one by one come to the cold wall that freezes; dark before their eyes; soul-lost and dead. (*He pours himself more wine.*) It's my belief the Universe is like a great prison and its deepest dungeon is the Earth, the scene of a man's life. Don't you agree? (*They all nod except for the corpse.*) Oh, you don't agree, Sire?

Ahikar No, he agrees. Don't you agree, Simeon? He's always been a close-mouthed man.

Anna And deafish. You're deafish, aren't you, Simeon?

Tobias *quickly pours* **Kanach** *another bowl of wine as he sits opposite the dead man.*

Kanach Brother Simeon, you remind me of my long dead friend, Warad. We fought in ten campaigns together. It seemed every grain of sand from here to the

Blue Nile was flecked with our blood. We saw such things
that turned the sky rusty till Warad didn't want to see
what the world had to show him any more. So he asked,
'Who took the song and broke it?' and sat on anthills. It
was too much trouble to get up. One day we found him
sitting on one, dead, his world-sick heart, cold. What do
you think of that story?

Simeon's corpse suddenly falls face down on the table.

Ahikar   Drunk.

Tobias   Dead drunk.

Kanach   No, just plain dead.

Tobias   You think he's dead?

Anna   Dead? Really? . . . No, no . . . But then again,
it'd be hard to tell with old Simeon.

Anna, Tobias *and* **Ahikar** *examine the body cautiously.*

Ahikar   Dead, you say?

Kanach   Stone-cold dead. If any fly, mouse or little
scaly thing dies I know it on the instance. You can't hide
death from me, it's my business. I calculate this one's my
wandering Jew.

He gets up.

Ahikar   Captain, I hope you don't believe a person of
my eminence would break the law?

Kanach   No, my lord. The law forbids burying dead
Jews. But there's nothing against inviting one home for
supper. However, I should report the matter to the
Courts of Justice. But a soldier has other laws to live by.
One of them is, if a man offers me free drink and
hospitality I never knowingly do him dirt . . . (*He picks up
the corpse.*) I shall deposit dead Simeon where he fell. And
place a guard on him else he starts wandering again.

He moves Upstage with the corpse.

Anna   Captain, as you are clearing up.

She opens the cupboard door Upstage Left and the other body falls out.

Kanach   Ah, a matching set . . . (**Tobias** *carries the second body over to him.*) Is that everyone?

Anna, Tobias *and* **Ahikar** *look at* **Tobit** *who nods.* **Tobias** *opens the front door for* **Kanach** *who tucks one corpse under his arm and carries the other over his shoulder. He pauses in the doorway for a moment and pointedly takes* **Tobit**'s *shovel before exiting.*

Tobias *shuts the door quickly.*

Anna   My heart shook.

Tobit   Why, Anna? The Lord looks after us. We are His children.

Anna   Oh, why can't we be someone else's children?!

Ahikar (*putting on his cloak*)   When I came to Court, the Lord of the Purse said, 'Ahikar, others will do it to you now, but if you bow low enough and crawl long enough, one day you will be able to do it to them in your turn.' I'll not miss my turn just to protect you, Uncle. I can think only of me and mine and I truly pity you and yours. I'll not come again. You are alone.

He exits Upstage Centre.

Anna   Terror and shadows seize us, we are lost on the rim of the world.

Tobit *kneels as the lights go down on him Downstage Centre.*

Tobit   A fool says what he knows, a wise man knows what he says. I know I must thank God for deliverance . . . King Sennacherib was riding outside the walls of Tyre when an enemy archer fired at him. A foot soldier shouted a warning and the arrow missed its mark. The king told the soldier to ask for any favour he pleased. The soldier said, 'Your Majesty, my captain keeps beating me, let me serve under another captain.' 'Idiot,' roared the

king, 'why didn't you ask to be made a captain yourself?!'
We are like that, Lord. We pray for the small needs of the
moment – for prosperity and peace. But we do not pray
for redemption.

Scene Two

Lights up on **Tobit**'s *garden. A bright sun shines on a broken
wall painted with flowers Stage Right.* **Tobit** *gets up as*
Anna *enters Stage Left with washing.*

Tobit   People are never satisfied. Winter is too cold,
summer too hot. But have you noticed nobody complains
about the spring?

He helps her lay the washing on top of the wall to dry.

Anna   This is the day spring turns to summer. Perhaps
it heralds a turn in our fortunes, Tobey? Winter's been
hard. Do you remember the time we were left without a
single drachma to buy food and sat shivering under a
blanket and I said, 'At least the people next door won't
smell my cooking and come round to cadge a meal.'

Tobit   And we both thought of your thick hot cabbage
soup.

Anna   Then there was a knock and the girl from next
door was standing there with a bowl saying, 'Can you
spare some of your cabbage soup, please?'

Tobit   Heaven help us, they could smell our thoughts.

Anna   Tobey, your father Tobeil, blessings-on-his-
name, was a man who feared the Lord God of Israel too
and kept the Commandments. But he never let it get in
the way of business. Remember how he used to sell
donkeys at rock-bottom prices? And how that Nubian
merchant couldn't believe it. 'I can't sell donkeys at your
prices, Tobeil, even after I've forced my farmers to give
me free fodder and my slaves to work without wages. So

how can you sell donkeys cheaper than me?' 'Simple,' says your father, 'you steal fodder and labour. I just steal donkeys.' . . . Everyone respected your father. My family thought you'd turn out like him, otherwise, they would never have agreed to our marriage.

Tobit You were so beautiful and I was so lucky.

Anna My dear, my dear, what shall I do with you?

They kiss.

Tobit Enjoy the bright day. From the abode of splendour He creates the bright sky, sun and singing birds up there . . . (*The shadow of birds flit above them.*) Solomon was thought the wisest of men because he could speak the language of birds. Their doings are a mystery known only to God Himself. In winter there's none in Nineveh, yet now the sky is filled with their song. Have they been asleep in caves and hollow trees or have they hidden in pairs at the bottom of lakes and rivers, wing to wing? Or did they follow the sun to Egypt? They are God's bright messengers, Anna, needing no other food but air and the dew of heaven.

As he looks up smiling, his face is covered with bird droppings. **Anna** *bursts out laughing as he cleans himself with a rag.*

Anna If those feathered filthies are truly God's messengers, I have a shrewd idea what He just said to you.

Tobit (*handing her the rag*) Clean out my eyes, my dear, if you would be so good.

Anna (*wiping his eyes*) They seem clean enough . . . What is it, Tobey?

Tobit I can't see.

Anna (*wiping his eyes again*) But there's no more bird stuff in them. Nothing.

Tobit Nothing's what I see . . . It's midnight for me
. . . Anna, I'm blind!

Anna Bird droppings can't make you blind . . . Rest
against the wall . . . (*She guides him so his back is against
the wall.*) What's happening, Tobey? I don't know what's
happening . . . Tobias will know . . . I'll fetch
Tobias! . . .

She rushes out Stage Left. **Tobit** *slowly slides down to sit at
the foot of the wall.*

Tobit You are just, oh Lord. Do not punish me for my
sins and needless faults. Remember me Lord and let me
see.

The **Archangel Raphael,** *in a dazzling white gown, comes
through the wall and stands beside him.*

Raphael I come from the dwelling-place of dew-breeze
in the centre of Heaven. My wings are the days of the year
and they cover the world. I have three hundred and sixty-
five thousand eyes and each eye is like a light.

Tobit Can you spare me two? Who are you?

Raphael I am Archangel Raphael, who looks on God's
face which is like iron made incandescent. Listen to the
sound of an angel.

He claps his hands together violently, but there is no sound.

Tobit I hear it! You are Raphael, clad in a garment of
light. The Lord has not abandoned me.

Raphael No, He has broken the watchtowers,
penetrated the empty spaces, placed Himself at the head
of all those stripped by oblivion . . . (*He suddenly goes
stiff, his right arm jerks rigidly upright, his forefinger
pointing to the sky like a lightning conductor.*) I hear you,
Lord . . . Oh . . . Ahh . . . (*He relaxes.*) Son Tobit, there
has been a mistake. I've never been beyond Ruha and the
four winds encircling Paradise before. It's my first
mission into this darkness and I hope my last. I only tell

the truth. But truth is a commodity rarely used here. The Lord says when in Assyria do as the Assyrians do. So I'm to travel through this world in disguise. Nobody's supposed to know who I am.

Tobit   I'm nobody, ask anybody. But I do know. You are Raphael, Archangel of the Lord, Healer and Bearer of Light. You told me. You can't not tell me. I can't now not know something I know.

Raphael   You can. We have to start again.

He gestures and **Tobit** *goes rigid.* **Raphael** *moves backwards through the wall, and* **Tobit** *slides down to sit in exactly the same place as before.*

Tobit   . . . Do not punish me for my sins and needless faults. Remember me, Lord, and let me see.

Raphael *reappears through the wall. His suit this time is still white but dusty.*

Raphael   Good day, Sire, I wish you happiness.

Tobit (*struggling up*)   Happiness comes hard now. I'm blind, cursed by the God of Abraham.

Raphael   He wields the universe as gamblers do dice. But He changes on a whim, I know him. I mean, I speak to Him when I pray . . . I'm Azarias, son of Ananias of Shephat.

Tobit   The great Ananias? I'm Tobit, son of Tobeil from Upper Galilee. I knew Ananias when I was a boy. A good man, he never strayed from the path of holiness. Is he well?

Raphael   Well and prosperous.

Tobit   We worshipped together. Yet God raises him up and plunges me into the dark. My eyes, Azarias, my eyes!

Raphael   Let me look at them. How did you go blind?

Tobit   A swallow shat on me from a great height.

Raphael   A swallow? That's a new one . . . Yes, the pupils are milky white. We can do nothing now except pray.

Anna *and* **Tobias** *hurry in Stage Right.*

Tobias   Father, can you see?

Tobit   No, all's still dark. We can only pray.

Anna   Pray? Would you pray to a God who treated His people so?

Raphael   Me? I'm not the right person to ask.

Tobit   Anna, this is Azarias, son of my old friend, Ananias. Brother Azarias, my wife and son, Tobias.

Tobias   What happened to your eyes?

Raphael   He was shat on from a great height. A high-flying swallow.

Tobias   This is hard. Reduced to poverty, threatened with death, now blinded. You must try not to do anything dangerous, Father, like getting up in the morning.

Anna   That wouldn't help. With his luck he'd be attacked by a rabid bedbug.

Tobit   At least I won't be able to bury any more dead Jews. That should please you, Anna?

Anna   Tobey, Tobey, it does. But how do we live now? You're blind and we've no money. You're the son of an old friend, Brother Azarias, can you help?

Raphael   No, I'm looking for work.

Anna   I should've guessed. Aren't there any rich Jews left?

Tobit   When I was Purveyor to King Shalmeneser, I left ten talents of silver with a kinsman in Media – Brother Gabael of Rhages.

Anna   Why didn't you get it back years ago?

Tobit If I had, I wouldn't be able to now when we need it most.

Tobias But you're blind, Father. You can't go and I don't know the way.

Raphael I do. I'll guide you.

Tobit And I'll pay you one drachma a day expenses.

Anna Wait, you're too trusting, Tobey. Who is this man? He says he's Azarias, but you've only his word for it. He could be lying.

Raphael I am not in the habit of lying, woman.

Anna I don't like the look of you. You've got a weak chin. And the eyes – shifty. You've got shifty eyes. Hasn't he got shifty eyes, Tobey?

Tobit How do I know? I can't see.

Tobias Mother's right. You do look odd.

Raphael How can I look odd? Heaven stands in my presence. I am the Lord's flame.

Anna You see, I'm right.

Tobias Yes, we have to be careful . . . You could be planning to rob me on the road.

Raphael Rob you? Of what? You've no money.

Anna His clothes. His person. You could be planning to sell our boy as a slave in Nubia.

Raphael Impossible, I don't think you could give him away.

Tobit We'll all go together, Azarias – just to calm my wife's fears.

Raphael Wrong. I go with Tobias, and you and your wife stay here. It's recorded in the book.

Tobias What book's that?

Raphael The Book of Tobit.

Anna This man is raving.

Tobit We go together or nobody goes.

Raphael That's worse . . . Oh, very well. We can adjust the record later. It doesn't have to be totally accurate. But let's go quickly, I'm already tired of this place, it has too many sharp eyes.

Anna There's a world of preparation before we can leave – food, clothes, offerings to God for a safe journey.

Raphael gestures. **Anna**, **Tobit** and **Tobias** 'freeze' and the wall is taken up to reveal a small handcart behind it full of provisions. **Anna**, **Tobit** and **Tobias** walk mechanically over to it.

Raphael Heaven is white, right and good. Dirt is down here. Every step men take leaves a black footprint. Flies carry it, black specks in the air. Every breeze is a vapour of slime. I came in white now I'm spotted over with filth. Dirt creeps into nostrils, mouth, every orifice filled with slush, grease and sweat. All creatures are grimed with dirt and these mortal, two-legged, two-eyed, fleshy bags of dung, are the dirtiest, Lord.

Scene Three

Raphael joins the others and gestures. He and **Tobias** pull the cart whilst **Tobit** and **Anna** walk alongside as they slowly cross Upstage.

Tobias Can you see anything, Father?

Tobit No. Once I was aware of God in splendour, now it's all dark, no meadows, streams, trees or mountains clothed in celestial light.

Raphael Yes, the green and the blue here is a wonder. Nature has no need of salvation. But isn't it the custom on journeys to tell stories?

Tobit Stories? The only stories I know are about my father, Tobeil. One day a neighbour called to borrow his donkey. 'I'm sorry,' said my father, 'I've already lent it to somebody else.' Unfortunately, at that moment his donkey started braying in the stable. 'But, Tobeil, I can hear the donkey,' said the neighbour. My father roared, 'A man who'd rather believe the word of a donkey than mine doesn't deserve to be lent anything.'

Tobit, **Anna** *and* **Tobias** *burst out laughing.*

Raphael But your father lied and a liar usurps God's prerogative and recreates the world in his own image.

Tobias It's a joke.

Raphael It's a lie.

Tobias There are lies and lies. Would you believe I lied if I told you I killed six unbelievers with one blow yesterday?

Raphael You?

Tobias Go look on our kitchen table back home. You'll find six unbelieving flies lying there next to the swatter. That was just one thwack. No lies about flies.

Anna *and* **Tobit** *laugh delightedly.*

Raphael Six unbelieving flies? I must find out if they were truly unbelieving. I'll ask the prophet Elijah, he'll know.

Anna No sense of humour. We're travelling with a man with a weak chin, shifty eyes and no sense of humour.

Raphael Humour's of the devil's party. I don't need it.

Anna We do. It's a precious balm for the suffering world.

Raphael Suffering ennobles.

Anna It embitters.

Raphael That depends how you use it.

Anna   You can't have suffered . . .

Tobias   Or you'd never have called Grandfather Tobeil of the devil's party. Remember how he came rushing out of our house one morning, stark naked?

Anna   He said that he'd been in such a hurry to get dressed, he forgot his clothes.

Tobias, Anna *and* **Tobit** *roar with laughter.*

Tobit   Let's rest by this pyramid.

Anna   There's no pyramid here, Tobey?

Tobit   There isn't? Oh, well, the sound and smell of these blossoms, birds and zephyrs are better than any pyramid.

Raphael   And the river. Don't forget the river over there.

As they stop Downstage Left, a broad ribbon of blue silk unrolls Upstage Right.

Anna   See if you can catch some fish, Tobias.

Tobias   There's no fish in these parts, mother.

Anna   Don't be so bone-lazy. Get up and try. And don't get into any mischief.

As she and **Tobit** *settle down by the side of the cart,* **Tobias** *and* **Raphael** *cross to Stage Left.*

Tobias   What mischief could I get into in the middle of nowhere? I suppose we all have to have parents? Do you like yours, Azarias?

Raphael   I can't recall. I was born out of God's forehead. I mean, I don't remember my parents.

Tobias   Mine still treat me like a child. And I'm the one holding the family together since my father started doing good works for God's sake, and being paid off in false coin. Look how he's been treated.

Raphael When King Nebuchadnezzar began to sing the praises of the Lord, an angel came down and slapped his face saying, 'You want to praise God while you are wearing your crown but now let me hear you praise Him after being slapped in the face.'

Tobias That's what I mean, the God of Israel is too fickle. He's dark, dangerous and bloodthirsty. I think He should lighten up. Frankly, the old fertility gods might suit me better – food, drink and women. I need fun.

Raphael Fun? What's fun?

Tobias What's fun? Where've you been living?

Raphael Heaven.

Tobias Heaven? Where's that?

Raphael (*gestures vaguely*) Back there . . . around Galilee . . .

Tobias Around Galilee?

They are standing on the edge of the band of blue silk and **Raphael** *quickly looks down into it.*

Raphael Do you see any fish?

Tobias No, I can see right to the bottom and there's no sign of any . . . (*He and* **Raphael** *turn back to* **Anna** *and* **Tobit**, *Stage Left.*) Mother, there's no fish here!

As he shouts, a rainbow-coloured fish of monstrous size leaps out from a hole in the silk. **Anna** *leaps up shrieking and pointing.* **Tobias** *and* **Raphael** *turn back but the fish has already disappeared back down the hole.* **Anna** *pulls a sleepy* **Tobit** *upright and starts dragging him to* **Tobias** *and* **Raphael**.

Anna Did you see that fish, Tobey?

Tobit No.

Anna It was huge. You must be blind.

Tobit Yes, I am.

Anna Oh, that's right . . . Tobias, a monster fish – in the air above your head!

Tobias A monster flying fish?

Anna I saw it, I tell you! It's down there.

They all peer down at the ribbon of blue silk.

Tobias We should be able to see it if it's as big as you say.

Anna It's bigger than that even.

Anna, Tobias *and* **Raphael** *simultaneously let out cries of fright as the monster fish suddenly shoots up out of its hole again. The three leap back in unison leaving* **Tobit** *standing alone on the edge of the silk, the fish flying above him.* **Tobias** *manages to pull him away as the fish plunges back into its hole.*

Anna Now do you believe?

Tobit I always believe – it's easier.

Raphael Tobias, you have to catch that fish.

Tobias Me?! How?

Raphael By the gills.

Tobias The gills?

Raphael Leave it to me.

Anna We'll have gefilte fish for a week from that little beastie.

Tobias But I haven't agreed.

Raphael Shhh, it's flying again.

He and **Tobias** *tense, as sure enough the great fish leaps out for a third time.* **Raphael** *whips out a cudgel from under his tunic and hits the fish on the head as it passes. As it falls,* **Tobias** *grabs it round the gills and flings it on the ground. They wrestle violently. The others shout and* **Raphael** *lashes out with his cudgel first hitting* **Tobias** *and then the* *fish. It lies still.* **Tobias** *disentangles himself and staggers up.* **Anna** *embraces him.*

Anna   I was so frightened for you, Tobias. You mustn't do it again.

Tobias   I didn't want to do it the first time.

Tobit   I couldn't see you, Son, but it sounded heroic.

Tobias   Yes, it was. It's huge, Father.

Tobit   Perhaps it's the Syrian fish goddess, Derceto?

Raphael   No, but it is unique.

At that moment a second huge fish pokes its head out of the hole, sees its dead companion, lets out a series of sad piercing cries and squirts a jet of water straight into **Raphael**'s *face before disappearing again.* **Anna** *and* **Tobias** *laugh.*

Anna   You see, you can be funny when you want to be.

They drag the fish over to the cart Downstage Right.

Raphael   Now gut it and salt what you can't eat.

Anna   I don't need to be told that, sonny. I've cooked more meals than you've had hot dinners.

The fish is up against the cart and **Anna** *starts preparing it.*

Raphael   Brother Tobit, your wife has a very fiery humour.

Tobit   There are two kinds of heat, Brother Azarias. Peppers burn but dull the appetite. Horseradish, on the other hand, sharpens it. My Anna's horseradish hot.

Raphael   Hhmm . . . Tobias, I suggest you keep the fish's gall, heart and liver.

Tobias   Why?

Raphael   Why? Why? Everybody keeps asking why? I never heard the word 'why' till I came here. Why? Because the gall, heart and liver have strong curative properties, that's why – particularly the liver, which is the source of life.

Tobias   If I hadn't asked, I wouldn't have known that.

Raphael   Brother Tobit, before we reach Rhages we might stop at Exbatama and visit your kinsman, Raguel.

Tobit   A good thought, Azarias.

Raphael   I have them all the time.

Anna   Don't encourage him, Tobey.

Raphael   Now we must strike out across the desert of Media to face the sun that burns, the furnace-winds that scorch – the sirocco, the ghlili, the knamin, the simmon . . . simmon . . . s-i-m-m-o-n . . . (*The light turns yellow and they all crouch, heads down, a wind blows fiercely, and the light darkens.*) Soon the world will be covered with sand, the sand that buried the Pshylei and the Chaldees, the sand that moves like molten sea, fills the mind, cuts into bone, creeps into every crevice, ears, eyes, nose, arse, mouth, the sand that covers earth, sky and the space between and makes the lost sand-ghosts dance and sing.

Indistinct **Shapes** *appear through the yellow light Upstage Left and Right chanting in high-pitched voices and dancing with lighted candles in their hands which do not flicker despite the wind.*

First Shape   I am I because you are you, and you are you because I am I. But that won't do. I am I because I am I, and you are you because you are you.

Second Shape   Why am I so empty? Why am I pale with fear? Because I never cried, never sighed. I thought there was nothing here worth a tear.

Third Shape   There were miracles under my chair. I didn't know they were lying there in the muck. So many, but I never saw any. I never bent down to pick them up.

The three **Shapes** *exit backwards Upstage as the wind dies away.*

Scene Four

Lights up on a large room in **Raguel***'s house. Coloured sheepskins hang from the Flies and round the walls. Table and chairs Stage Left, door Stage Right and double doors Upstage Centre. The 'baa-baaing' of sheep can be heard in the distance as* **Raguel** *formally embraces* **Tobit, Tobias, Anna** *and* **Raphael***.*

Raguel   Sheep, sheep, nothing but sheep covering the hills and the valleys, fat sheep's eyes following you everywhere. Did you see 'em? All mine. They say herding sheep is nothing to do and all day to do it in. There's more to it than that, believe me. Any of you know anything about sheep?

Raphael   Elijah told a story that one day he was forced to begin the sabbath in an open field with a flock of sheep. When he started to pray all the sheep rose on their hind legs and stayed there, looking at him till he finished.

Raguel   My sheep would never do that – too stupid. Mind you if they did I could make a fortune out of 'em . . . You, sir, you look like a man called Azarias. Azarias of Galilee. Are you related?

Raphael   I am Azarias.

Raguel   No wonder you look like him. I'm glad you and your family broke your journey to visit us, Brother Tobit . . .

As they cross to sit at the table, **Tobit** *falls over a pile of sheepskins.*

Raguel   Brother Tobit, I couldn't help but notice how you came into the room just now, by falling through the window. I'm only guessing but can it be you're blind?

Anna   Of course he's blind. He was shat on from a great height.

Raguel   Painful.

Tobit   The Lord God of Israel saw fit to shower me with afflictions.

Raguel   He's showered me too since I left Galilee – money, houses, land and sheep, drachmas on the hoof.

Tobias   You must be a great worshipper of God of Israel for Him to reward you so.

Raguel   I'd like to be but I haven't had the time. I leave the God-part to my daughter, Sarah.

Anna   I don't understand. You aren't a strict worshipper of the Lord like my husband – good thoughts, good words, good deeds, good conscience, loyal as fine gold, whole as an egg. Yet, he's poor and blind and you're rich and successful. Why? Master Azarias, you say you're in close touch with the Lord, can you explain why?

Raphael   There's that word again, 'why?' It's a matter of faith. True faith lies beyond questions and comes only after it has been challenged.

Raguel   It's a mystery, as deep as why sheep get blue-tongue, sore muzzle and pulpy kidneys. I'm a normal backslider but Sarah serves the Lord with a full heart sleeping and waking, sunrise, sunset. And look at her reward.

Tobias   She's blind too!

Tobit   That's hard for a young girl.

Anna   When the wind blows the blind are helpless, even the best.

Raguel   No, she's not blind. It's worse. When she reached marriageable age, I gave her a large dowry. My motto is if you have it, let others see you have it, otherwise what's the point of having it? Of course, there was no difficulty finding a bridegroom – Abishai, son of David, the biggest goat farmer in these parts. Goats're the coming thing. They stink but they're less trouble than sheep. The wedding was the most expensive ever seen in this part of Media. One hundred and fifty-four guests and they didn't stop eating and drinking for two days. Afterwards, Sarah and Abishai retired to the bridal chamber. Next morning we went in to greet the newly-weds as is the custom and found Sarah asleep, fully dressed on the bed and Abishai cold dead beside her. When she woke up, she could remember nothing.

Anna   The groom's ardour proved too strong; his passionate heart burst imagining the fleshy delights to come. It's a sad business for you, Master Raguel, but my Tobit lost two eyes, you only lost a bridegroom.

Raguel   Seven.

Tobit   Seven? You lost seven bridegrooms?

Tobias   Isn't that careless?

Raguel   Abishai was only the first. Sarah married again . . . and again . . . and again. Seven times a widow and still a virgin. And I've got seven graves out there to prove it.

Tobit   You might take me to them later. I'm always interested in well-dug graves.

Anna   Please, Tobey, not here!

Tobias   They all died on their bridal nights?

Raguel   Died, stone dead. And all young too. Except the last, Joshua Mordecai the Tanner, seventy years old last counting. We were lucky to get him. Though I'd doubled the dowry, word had spread. You can understand the difficulty in recruiting new husbands for my Sarah. Where is she? She should be here to greet guests. I'll see what's amiss.

He hurries out Stage Left.

Anna   You can't tell me that girl's totally innocent. She's doing something wrong in the bedroom, sending all those men to Abraham's bosom when they should be in hers.

Raphael   It's not Sarah but the demon Asmodeus, Asmodeus of the First Hierarchy. He's in love with the girl, and so jealous he kills anyone who tries to touch her.

Anna   First the prophet Elijah, now the demon Asmodeus – you seem to know everybody.

Raphael   Though a demon, Asmodeus is still a full Seraphim, so it's natural I'd know him. Just as I know Tobias will be the eighth bridegroom of Sarah.

Tobias   Never.

Raphael   I know the seas, the lands and the secrets. Look into my eyes. See, God wants Tobias to marry Sarah.

Tobit   I can't see, I'm blind.

Raphael   Still look.

They look into **Raphael**'s *eyes.*

Anna   God doesn't shine in a one-drachma-a-day man.

Tobit   He's my son. God won't demand such a sacrifice.

Tobias   Don't fret. I'll not marry this woman, not never, ever . . . (*Low.*) It's plain she's so ugly she frightened the seven to death. I know the kind – a face you should charge money to nail a board over. Bald as a bat, no teeth . . .

Anna   Why're you whispering, I've heard she's deaf too.

Raguel *hurries back, Stage Left.*

Raguel   Sarah's coming.

He opens the doors Upstage Centre. **Sarah** *approaches under a dazzling blue sky, dressed in a shepherd's smock and singing as a chorus of unseen sheep accompany her with gentle 'baa-baaing'.*

Sarah (*singing*)   'Young lambs, young lambs, young lambs to sell. / Who would cry young lambs, young lambs, young lambs to sell? / If we had as much money as

we could tell. / Who would cry young lambs, young
lambs, young lambs to sell?'

Tobias *and* **Sarah** *stare at each other*.

Tobias   Amo.

Sarah   Amas.

Tobias   Amat.

Sarah   Ovunque io mi sia, io sono Anore.

Tobias   Ahime! Che de tutti gli humani effetti solo è
amore insatiabile. A l'amour on resiste en vain.

Sarah   Amour, dont les amants savent seuls le mystère.

Tobias   Master Raguel, I ask for the hand of your
daughter, Sarah, in marriage.

Anna *cries out, and* **Tobit** *jumps up, knocking over a chair*.

Raguel   Tobias, as kinsman, I must give my daughter to
you as proscribed by custom and the Book of Moses.
Kinsmen cannot refuse marriage 'cept on grounds of
poverty or madness.

Anna   He has both, my son's arse and brains're hanging
out. When he was a child he liked digging holes and filling
them in and setting fire to his clothes.

Tobit   When he's said 'hello', he's told you all he knows.

Anna   He still thinks assets are baby donkeys.

Raguel   That means he's plain stupid not stark mad.
But though Moses says I must accept him, ties of blood
make me refuse. The risk is too great.

Anna   Thank you, Brother Raguel.

Tobias   Then I ask again for the hand of your daughter,
Sarah, in marriage.

Sarah   When I see him, Father, straight jumps the
quick of my heart and the ocean's roar is a tinkling bell to
me; time stops and paradise springs up where he is. I so
deeply love him, Father, I can no longer call my soul my

own. Love is the root from which the wonders of God shine forth, so I beg you, Father, don't let me marry the man I love else he die. Refuse him!

Tobias   A love that's afraid of a little danger isn't worth the name of love. Besides, love conquers death.

Anna   Not in the last seven fights it hasn't.

Tobit   I'll sacrifice an ox, cock and lamb on God's hard altar, but not my son.

Anna   He is my babe. Let God feel these heartfelt tears.

Raphael   If God had feelings, He too would grow old. Like Abraham, you must sharpen the sacrificial knife. This is no game for the weak and the cowardly. Faith and the abyss are next to each other – one within the other.

Tobias   This isn't a matter of faith but money. Master Raguel, if you defy the Book of Moses, your reputation amongst fellow Israelities will suffer. If your own people distrust you, the rest will soon follow. Your sheep will die on the hoof, their wool rot on their backs.

Raguel   My sheep at risk?

Tobias   All's at risk. This may be your last chance. The seven dead grooms are no secret. No one else is going to risk being number eight. Sarah will be left unmarried and who'll be your heirs? Accept and you'll live on in our children. Refuse and your line ends here.

Raguel   I accept.

Sarah   Father, I sleep with the chill of death beside me. Don't condemn my love!

Raguel   I must. Tobias, you have my daughter's hand in marriage.

Tobit   This is bitter.

Anna   I'll not live!

She rushes out sobbing, Stage Right.

Tobit   Tobias, go comfort your mother.

Tobias *hurries out, Stage Right.*

Raphael   Save me from these petty concerns. I've grasped universes. I was there when the Lord fought the first battle against darkness and the sky filling with banners of light, trumpets of truth. But God walks invisible through time and forgets. I'm sent down to this dungeon, slurred by questions, mired by doubts. Look what's become of my lovely white robes. Filthy . . . absolutely filthy!

He exits Upstage Centre.

Raguel   He must be a prophet, I can't understand a word he says . . . I'm sorry, Sarah, I think I've done the wrong thing again. That's why I like sheep. They're even more stupid than me.

Sarah   Go to them, Father. They'll make you feel better.

Raguel   Yes, I can hear them calling. I'm coming, boys, baa-baa-baaaa . . . baa-baa-baaaa . . .

He exits Upstage Centre.

Sarah   There's no easy way. But my spirit is indestructible, like the sun which seems to set but really shines on and on unceasing. Dealing in death I eat life. I'm a tree and God is my rain.

Tobit   I see your strength. Help me. I've doubts so dense they tear the night. I try to move towards God but He moves away from me.

Sarah   When I was small my father taught me how to walk by standing in front of me and holding out his hands on either side so I couldn't fall. But the moment I staggered closer, he'd move back and held his hands further apart. He'd do it again and again, so in the end I could walk alone.

The light fades down as night falls.

Sarah } *(singing)* 'From the Heaven of Heavens to
Tobit } the Dark Clouds. / From the Dark Clouds to
the Abode. / From the Abode to the Dwelling-
Place. / From the Dwelling-Place to the Skies.
/ From the Skies to the Plains. / From the
Plains to the Depths who can be compared to
you, Lord, / Who is Your equal? . . .'

All lights out as **Sarah** *and* **Tobit** *continue singing in the
darkness.*

Scene Five

An unseen **Chorus** *takes up the singing, Upstage Centre as
a bridal procession approaches in the darkness with lights on
the end of long poles.* **Tobias** *and* **Sarah** *walk under a
canopy held up by* **Tobit, Raguel, Raphael** *and* **Anna.**
Rabbi Baanah *leads the procession strewing their path
with myrtle and barley.*

Chorus *(singing)* 'Take care of the bride. / Take care of
the bride. / See her ride the white stallion covered in
gold. / Her light is the light of morning. / Dawning in
splendour. / Dawning in splendour.'

As the procession pauses at the door of **Raguel**'s *house, light
comes up on the interior to show a bridal meal has just been
laid on the table.*

Baanah *sprinkles salt in the doorway and throws a live
chicken over his shoulder.*

The party enters. **Tobias** *stands Stage Centre whilst*
Anna, Raguel, Tobit, Baanah *and* **Raphael** *clap and*
Sarah *circles him three times.* **Tobias** *gives her his mantle,
girdle and hat.*

Baanah Thus the groom gives his bride, mantle, girdle
and hat to signify that his wife now shares his property
. . . The fish! Where's the fish? . . .

Raguel *quickly takes a fish from the table and puts it on the floor in front of* **Sarah** *and* **Tobias**.

That fish is grilled! It's supposed to be raw. Surely you've performed this ceremony enough times over the last year? . . . Oh, leave it . . . Tobias. Sarah. Jump . . . (**Tobias** *and* **Sarah** *jump over the fish*.) By so jumping we increase the fertility of the bride and the virility of the groom, who will be blessed with sons and daughters – if he should live that long . . . (**Raguel** *passes round bowls of wine from the table*.) Now is the time of joy and laughter as we drink to the health and prosperity of the newly-weds.

All drink except **Raphael**. *They cross to the table and sit in silence*.

Tobit An angel must be passing overhead.

Raphael Closer than that.

Baanah *pours himself more wine*.

Baanah I'll stay the night, Master Raguel. You'll be needing my services again tomorrow for the funeral.

Tobit God will protect my son, Rabbi.

Baanah You're a stranger here, Master Tobit, otherwise your son wouldn't be seated where he is. Sarah's a good girl but everything she touches turns to rigor mortis. In my experience many bridegrooms go into the bridal chamber young and healthy and come out corpses, but rarely literally, as they do here. More wine.

Anna I spent the day on the floor covered with ashes, praying that the eyes of my husband and son would be opened. But they're still blind. Tobias, turn away before it's too late. Divorce her. There's nothing shameful there. Your father and me were divorced.

Tobias I didn't know that.

Tobit According to the Babylonian Talmud, a Jew should divorce his wife after ten years if she's childless. Your mother was childless, so in the tenth year of marriage, I divorced her according to the book, and remarried her on the same day.

Anna   A year later you were born. What more proof do you need? Divorce her, Tobias, or tomorrow morning you'll wake up and find yourself dead.

Tobias   How can I divorce her, I've only just married her. Don't talk of it. I'm surprised it's such a small wedding feast, Master Raguel.

Raguel   I didn't invite more because they wouldn't've come. Too painful for them. Most families in these parts have lost a relative, marrying Sarah.

Raphael   God tries the hearts of men and women to see whose heart beats for Him. He probes wounds to find such hearts.

Baanah (*drinking*)   Don't tell me what God is doing. That's my job. I'm the priest here. I'm the only one qualified to be in touch with the Creator. I trained for it. You're just another bumble-footed prophet. Israel's plagued with your kind. No wonder the Lord's angry with His people. Who'd like to be prayed to by an army of dank prophets like you, all gloom, doom and cold farfel? Do you know the real sin of our forefathers in the desert? It wasn't rebellion but melancholy. We're a melancholy people, Master Azarias. One must enjoy life in spite of life. Look at this wedding – the wine's good but not a sign of fiddles or fun.

Sarah   Rabbi Baanah's right. We must rejoice in the Lord. Eden's wide open. Nothing bars us from it but ourselves.

Tobit   Put on a merry face though you may be crying.

Raguel   When my sheep are troubled and they baa-baa-baa, panpipes, flutes and songs send them skipping.

Anna   So they go more easily to slaughter.

Tobias   We've no fiddles or cymbals but we still sing and dance.

He and **Sarah** *bang the table rhythmically.* **Raguel** *plays on his Jew's harp.*

Sarah (*singing*)   'Winter is gone, gone, gone is my sorrow. / Laugh today though you weep, weep tomorrow.'

Sarah *and* **Tobias** *dance as all except* **Raphael** *join in singing.*

All (*singing*)   'Don't be afraid, drink, drink the cup dry. Let your heart blossom, don't ever sigh, / Don't ever sigh . . .'

Tobit *staggers up, drags* **Anna** *to her feet and they dance clumsily.*

All (*singing*)   'Winter is gone, gone, gone is my sorrow. / Laugh today though you weep, weep tomorrow.'

Anna *suddenly shrieks.* **Tobias** *and* **Sarah** *have sneaked away Stage Right during the dance.*

Anna   She's snatched him into darkness. Tobey, Tobey, we'll never see your brightlin' boy again!

Raguel   I wish I could've had it different. But he's a kinsman, I had no choice.

Anna   When men do their worst, they say they had no choice. He was so young, so fair, why cast him down?

Baanah   It's the way of things. Seawater casts up mud and filth but bright coral is cast down into the depths. Only Heaven has a true balance.

Raphael   Sometimes not even there. You'll find some odd judgements amongst the ten ranks of angels in the seven Heavens, I can tell you. Why is that shlemiel, Shemuel, a chief seraphim? Why was Shakziel made angel of water insects, and Serahal, angel of trees not bearing fruit? Surely they deserved better? Why expel the two angels who told of Sodom's destruction and yet not punish the one who killed a priest in the temple? It doesn't make sense. Injustice, it seems, is built into the fabric even of heaven. And my garment grows dirtier by the moment.

He exits Stage Right.

Baanah   If I could sing I'd force God to live amongst men. But I can't. I'm like a blacksmith who bought an anvil, hammer and bellows and goes to work but nothing happens. The forge remains cold. I have everything I need except the spark. It's why I must have more wine, more wine!

Raguel   'Baa-baa', do you hear my sheep? They're stupid but sensitive with it. They sense our crying and despair.

Anna   We should've warned our boy of love.

Tobit   We've had too much of words. We've said it all. So let's sit, join hands and hearts and plead silently with the Lord of Heaven, for silent prayer is the most eloquent.

Hands touching, they stare straight ahead, praying silently and with great intensity. **Baanah** *suddenly pitches forward onto the table, dead drunk. The others continue. A shadow passes over them as the lights fade out and an unseen* **Chorus** *intones the Burial Kaddish.*

Chorus (*singing*)   'Magnified and sanctified be His Great Name in the world that is created anew when He will revive the dead and raise them up into life eternal . . .'

Scene Six

Lights up on **Sarah**'s *bedroom. The bed Stage Right with a small table, lighted candle and full-length mirror beside it Downstage Right. Door Upstage Centre.*

Sarah *and* **Tobias** *face each other as the Burial Kaddish continues softly over.*

Tobias If I were a spear, I'd hurl myself into your side.

Sarah If I were a tent and you were in me, we'd warm ourselves with desire.

Tobias If I were a child and you were my nurse, I'd suckle your breasts and quench my thirst.

Sarah If I were a tongue and you were my words, I'd sing love songs of joy . . . Oh Tobias, since I woke to find death so close, so often, my senses are now sprung-fresh. We'll not lie in the ground before our time but leap up like trumpet blasts and embrace this world which is so full and fair.

They embrace. There is a knock on the door. The Burial Kaddish stops immediately as **Sarah** *runs across to the bed and hides under the sheets.* **Tobias** *opens the door and* **Raphael** *enters.*

Tobias Azarias, this is my wedding night. Have you no sense of occasion?

Raphael None. You'll soon be about your business. Man has a very small organ, the more he feeds it, the more he needs to – and vice versa. I'm here to give you some liver.

He takes out a small pouch.

Tobias Liver? I'm not hungry. Are you hungry, Sarah?

Sarah Not for liver.

Raphael It's not to eat. It's the liver we took from the great fish. I told you it had certain curative properties. (*He puts the pouch on the small table next to the candle.*) When the demon Asmodeus appears, burn this liver on the candle flame.

Tobias Why?

Raphael Why? Why? Why? Why? Why do you all have to ask 'why' when every 'why' has a 'therefore'? It's all questions down here. You'll be asking me next does Mount Sinai know where Moses is, and do fleas have navels?

Sarah Do they?

Raphael That's not my department. I'm not here to talk of fleas' navels but to protect Tobias. Though why he's protected is another mystery.

Tobias I understand, Master Azarias.

Raphael So what are you going to do with the liver when the demon appears?

Sarah Fry it.

Tobias With onions.

Raphael No! Don't fry it with onions, just burn it. And quick. Don't let him talk, demons can be very persuasive. We used to call Asmodeus, 'Old Silver-Tongue'.

Tobias Excellent. And so good night.

He bundles **Raphael** *out, shuts the door behind him and crosses back to the bed.*

Sarah Is Azarias a relative?

Tobias Never. My father knew his father in Jerusalem. He's touched, the sun's sucked dry one side of his brain.

Sarah Liver or no liver, he's right on one matter. You must take care tonight, my love.

As they embrace passionately, there is another knock on the door. **Tobias** *leaps off the bed and opens it.* **Anna, Tobit** *and* **Baanah,** *with a bottle, rush in.*

Tobit Is my son still alive?

Baanah It's hard to tell in this light.

Anna He's alive. You are alive, aren't you, Son, not a hollow shell possessed by demons?

Tobias   I'm alive.

Sarah   Good evening.

Anna   There's nothing good about it, madam. Tobias, I have the answer. Bridegrooms were only killed when they were about to make love to your bride. So you must abstain.

Tobit   Listen to your mother, Tobias. She could be right. The Lord of Israel is hard on lust, saying a man's shame is between his legs . . .

Baanah   And a fool's is between his cheeks. I tell you, Tobias, caress the breasts of this lovely girl all night, kiss her lips all day, spurn those who chide you for loving, eat and drink, laugh and clap your hands, enjoy the delights of this world which the Lord made for all to share whilst they can. (*He produces a dead cockerel.*) This bird will keep you safe. I whirl round and spatter its blood . . . round . . . round . . .

He whirls round the room with the dead cockerel.

Tobit   What's he doing?

Sarah   Dancing round with a dead cock.

Tobias   It's about as useful as throwing beans at a wall.

Baanah   Beans at a wall? Let's try that next. More wine first! I know the holy stuff and I tell you Solomon's father, old Teah was a drunkard and the brothers who pulled off Noah's little coloured shirt and sold it to the Philistines for gold and then went and bought barrels of cold borscht and kraplach in Egypt were drinkers and Nebuchadnezzy celebrated with 'em, oh yes, he used to guzzle wine straight from the jar and Balaam's ass was drinking wine, too, and Abraham stood behind the door holding his head and groaning after a heavy bout; they were all drunkards every last one of 'em . . .

He crashes to the floor dead drunk.

Tobias   He's drunk.

Baanah (*looking up*) Of course I'm drunk. I wouldn't act like this if I were sober, would I?

He falls forward again.

Tobias   Take him out.

Anna   But this may be the last time we shall ever see you, Tobias.

Tobit   I can't even see him now.

Tobias   You know the sun will rise tomorrow, Father, and so will I.

He embraces **Anna** *and* **Tobit**.

Sarah   Know if your son dies, I'll die. I can't live without him.

Crying, **Anna** *and* **Tobit** *embrace her.*

Baanah   I love you all too and coming from me, that's a compliment . . . Beans! . . . where are the beans for the wall? . . .

Anna *and* **Tobit** *carry him out. As* **Tobias** *thankfully closes the door behind them and starts back to the bed, there is another knock.* **Tobias** *opens it in a fury to find* **Raguel** *standing in the doorway.* **Sarah** *rushes over.*

Sarah   What is it, father?

Raguel   All my sheep are tucked in for the night. So I came to see if you were still up.

Tobias   And active which I was about to prove if you hadn't knocked.

Raguel   You're a fine looking lad, Tobias. (*Moving round him.*) Taller than I thought . . . broader, too . . . and heavier.

Tobias   Big bones. I've always had big bones.

Suspicious, **Sarah** *has looked round the doorway and produces a shovel* **Raguel** *has left concealed outside.*

Sarah   What's this for, Father?

Raguel I thought I'd do some summer planting.

Sarah At this time of night?

Tobias My father suffers from the same disease. Our families must be descended from a long line of gravediggers.

Sarah Father, Tobias isn't dead yet.

Raguel Of course not. I couldn't sleep, so I thought I'd do something useful. Just in case.

Tobias Then do it quietly, please. It can be disturbing hearing someone digging your grave outside the bedroom window on your wedding night . . .

He shepherds **Raguel**, *shuts the door behind him and goes back to the bed with* **Sarah**.

Sarah It won't be needed, will it, Tobias? But all those men struck down. I ask myself, is there something wrong in me?

Tobias *puts on his night-shirt in front of the mirror.*

Tobias That's a question I've asked too. All my life I never got results, only consequences. In Babylon they say if I became an undertaker, people would stop dying. All my paths have been wrong ones till I met you.

Sarah Aren't you afraid this is a wrong one too?

Tobias No, I'm only afraid of life without you, and what the night may bring.

He crosses to the bed and they hug each other but a figure remains reflected in the mirror. **Tobias** *and* **Sarah** *kiss and there is yet another knock.*

As they both look up exasperatedly at the door, the figure steps out of the mirror. It is the demon, **Asmodeus**, *with a white face and dressed in yellow Japanese robes. He resembles* **Raphael** *as he gestures and* **Sarah** *falls back unconscious.*

Asmodeus   'Let there be light,' God said and there was, just a little. But even He lacked the power to light more than a small corner of infinity. There are worlds of darkness left as if He hasn't spoken. One guttering candle flame of light in a universe of darkness.

Tobias   Who are you?

Asmodeus   When I was a child, I asked my mother Lilith, 'Who are human beings?' 'The offal of the universe, the scum of Creation,' she said. 'You see, God delegated the making of this world to a minor demigod and then forgot about it. Look at the result.' 'What do human beings do?' I asked. 'Evil, Asmodeus, nothing but evil. Stay clear of them,' she replied. Good advice but I'm a demon and I never take good advice, even from my mother.

Tobias   What are you doing here?

Asmodeus   Indulging in sin. I've fallen in love with a human being. Though I hate the light, I marvel at her soul which shines so bright. I can hear my mother say, 'Asmodeus, demons do not love.'

Tobias   Where did you come from?

Asmodeus   The other side of the mirror. There's a world compressed there, forced to repeat and repeat the actions of men and women, all things negative to your positive. If you look deep into mirrors, you'll see silent armies standing ready to break through with Cain, Essau, Korah, Dartha and the Planets leading, swords unsheathed, banners unfurling.

Tobias   Lord save us.

Asmodeus   You have it wrong, praying to a demigod who disobeyed orders and created this vile world. Its manifest imperfections prove its creator's inferiority to the true God, don't you think?

Tobias   How can I think? I'm too frightened.

Asmodeus We demons are frightened too – of men. What creature in the universe isn't? Such malignant bundles of rage, hate and murder, you even frighten demons. But you don't shout and scream like your seven predecessors did. They made loud guttering noises with their mouths. Are you going to make guttering noises?

Tobias No, my throat's too dry.

Admodeus Good, but just in case.

He gestures and **Tobias** *'freezes' in position.* **Asmodeus** *looks intently at* **Sarah** *and gestures again.* **Sarah** *wakes.*

Sarah Asmodeus.

Asmodeus A light once reeled loose from your bright flesh. Gone now. You're changed. I come to your room every night to wonder, so I know. Your pure soul's turned cloudy. Once it thrust through to the harmony above the Eighth Sphere exulting God with a sweet voice and yearning for the Light of Lights as on the first day of the Creation. I heard in you the silence of Heaven where worlds are created. That's gone too, now.

Sarah Are you going to kill Tobias, like you killed the others?

Asmodeus I sent them to darkness and silence. Demons call that bliss.

Sarah Why?

Asmodeus Why? The infernal 'why'. You never asked before. I sent them out of fear. It's why most killings are done. My day is passing, Sarah. Soon I won't be needed, men carry their own private demons with them. Nature eliminates the superfluous and we'll fade. I'm already fading, Sarah. I watched and watched too long. This is my last journey. When I go back into the mirror, come with me. You've searched so long for God. But you won't find Him in this world. As He had no part in its Creation, there's no trace of Him here. But come with me in darkness and in silence and you'll find Him there, guarded by four creatures and each creature has four faces and each face looks towards the sunrise.

Sarah   Once I would've come, I loved God alone, but now that love is shared with Tobias.

Asmodeus   That's why you've changed. Love has drawn you down into brute nature, making you like the rest. How far are you gone? (*He gestures,* **Tobias** *moves.*) When my hand falls, you die, Tobias.

Sarah   No, don't let your hand fall, Asmodeus. Take the light from me, not from my love.

Asmodeus   You never pleaded for the others, Sarah. Love has changed us both. As the dark was seized with greed for the brightness that appeared, so I was dazzled by your soul-light, hoping we could gaze together into the eyes of the Lord, shining like the first sun. But your light was shadowed and lies flowed like water. You've shrunk and there's nothing left but the song of Asmodeus' going. (*Singing.*) 'Hoost, hoost, oncairry. Annee, annee, alakanee. Ruel, ruel, ramock ruel. Annee, annee, yowl, yowl . . .'

As he sings **Tobias** *sidles over to the small table, takes the dried liver from the pouch to put on the candle flames, but is trembling so hard, he drops it on the floor.*

Asmodeus   Can I help? . . . (*He picks up the liver.*) Ah, the Archangel Raphael has been telling you how much I dislike the smell of burning liver. We were friends once above the Eighth Sphere. At one time, angels and demons were close, God and Satan one, that was before the Great Division. Few remember it now . . . I can no longer stand the stench of human beings. I leave you to your own demons. They'll make certain darkness gains the final victory, and the memory of mankind will be nothing but the nightmare of the unknown God, dreaming in eternal night. Good times ahead. Good times . . .

Asmodeus *gestures.* **Tobias** *and* **Sarah** *fall back in the bed and lie motionless. He puts the liver in the flame and as it*

*gives off thick smoke, he vanishes into the mirror amid the
sound of bells in reverse.*

At that moment the door Upstage Centre bursts open, and
Anna, Tobit, Baanah, Raphael *and* **Raguel** *rush in.*

Anna   Tobias!

Raguel   Where did this smoke come from?

Tobit   Somebody's been frying liver.

Raguel   At this time of night?

Anna   Perhaps they were hungry?

Raphael   No, I told Tobias it would protect him.

Anna   Fried liver?!

Raguel   Sarah!

Anna   Tobey, Tobey, their flesh is cold and marble
white.

Tobit   I can't hear their hearts beat.

Baanah   Because they're dead.

Raguel   Our ewes are dead.

Anna   If I were a bird, I'd fly to them so they could see
my tears.

Specks of grey ash fall.

Raguel ⎫ *(singing)* 'Seven boards to lay them on, such
Baanah ⎬ is the pain of death. / White robes to clothe
Anna ⎭ him in, as the cold rain falls. / Seven days of
      weeping, for they are newly wed. / Seven
      days of weeping, weeping for the dead . . .'

Raphael   Heaven bends, eternity crumbles. It can't be.
I was told they would live. I've been tricked. Why're you
silent, Tobit?

Tobit   I'm not. See, I open my mouth wide – I'm
screaming. When a man has reason to scream but can't,
that's the most terrible scream of all. But that's not for us.

We must sing a new song . . . An Assyrian tax collector asked Isaac if he owned the house he was living in. But Isaac didn't understand the language and his wife wrongly translated the question. 'He wants you to sing him a song,' she said. So Isaac warbled a psalm, but when the tax collector lost his temper and started beating him, his wife shouted, 'He doesn't like it, Isaac, give him another one, sing him a new song . . .' (*Singing.*) 'Never say you've reached the end. / That eternity will crumble and Heaven bend. / A new day will arrive. / And we survive, Lord, we survive.'

All (*singing*) 'The morning sun will dry our tears. / Dispel the pain of bitter years. / Our spirits too will revive. / And we survive, Lord, we survive.'

Tobias and Sarah sit up and join in.

Sarah } (*singing*) 'Our spirits too will revive. / And
Tobias } we survive, Lord, we survive.'

The grey ash turns into a glittering multicoloured shower as the others hug the young couple joyfully.

Anna Tobias! Sarah! You've been playing tricks. What happened?

Sarah I slept and dreamed of a lost world I can't remember.

Tobias I can't remember either. But I bested the demon.

Raphael How do you know that if you can't remember?

Tobias I'm alive, aren't I?

Raguel This calls for more wine.

Baanah Just a small one, Master Raguel.

They hurriedly exit Upstage Centre.

Raphael I knew my fried liver would send Asmodeus running.

Anna Your fried liver? Why don't you give credit where credit's due? It was my Tobias. He's a hero.

Sarah The best kind – a live one.

Tobias I did what I had to do. Whatever it was.

Baanah *and* **Raguel** *return Upstage Centre with some wine and drinking bowls.*

Raguel Baa-baa-baa, can you hear them offering congratulations? Listen to the lilt in their baa-baa-baaing. Sheep are very sensitive. They know the curse of the Raguels has been lifted.

Baanah A toast, blessings to the young bride and groom.

They drink.

Tobit Blessings too on the Lord God of Israel from whom all such blessings flow.

Anna And not before time. Our God loves everybody but from a distance. This is the least He could do for God-fearing Israelites and still one of the best is blinded.

Baanah Lord take pity on us. All we ask is to live out our lives in happiness and grace and drowning in wine.

Anna How did you get to be such a drunkard, Rabbi Baanah?

Baanah I always start with the intention of taking one drink. But one drink makes a new man of me and the new man wants a drink too. Now, everyone knows when two Jews get together, it's permissible they share a little wine. Anyway, after a few toasts to each other we both feel joyous. And remember on joyous occasions a Jew is *supposed* to drink!

Raguel And this is a joyous occasion. Tobias, I give you half of all I own. And when I die, the other half is yours. You're rich in sheep, oxen, donkeys, good clothes and sheep.

Tobias Thank you, Father-in-law. Now I want to return to Nineveh and flaunt it.

Sarah I long to flaunt it with you.

Anna We could hold a real wedding feast there, son. Let's return today or sooner.

Tobit But we still haven't collected the money Gabael of Rheges owes me.

Anna Master Azarias, you can finally make yourself useful. Tobey, give him the family seal to present to Brother Gabael, so he can collect the money.

Raphael Me collect money, madam?!

Tobit Don't be nervous. We trust you.

Anna Almost.

Tobias It's the quickest way. Otherwise, it'll take us an extra five days.

Raphael You mean I'll be down here another five days? Give me that seal!

Raguel I'll come with you to Nineveh – the sheep can spare me.

Baanah I can recommend some hostelries on the road with excellent wine cellars.

Baanah, Raguel, Tobias and **Anna** *exit Upstage Centre* as **Tobit** *gives* **Raphael** *a small seal.*

Tobit Master Azarias, give this to Brother Gabael and he'll know you come from me. We'll meet in Nineveh. Sister Sarah, guide me to the others.

Sarah Here's my hand.

Tobit Are you sad?

Sarah No, happy.

Tobit I see another colour in your voice.

Sarah Once I was Cain-marked for Israel. Unknown armies clashed over me. Light, darkness, life, death and the great questions of the higher sphere swirled about me then. I had been chosen. I loomed! Now there are no special signs about me, contentment has done its work. I feel a dwindling down. I am diminished by happiness. And the sound of bells grows fainter and the words float away forever . . . hoost . . . hoost . . . annee . . . annee . . .

As they exit Upstage Centre, the lights go down to a spot on **Raphael**, *standing Downstage Right looking at the seal.*

Raphael I'm Raphael, one of the seven archangels, second-in-command under Michael, with the tablet in my breast bearing the sacred name of God and I end up slimed on earth the lowest of the low – a palsied debt collector! My clothes grow blacker. Let's have an end to it quick. (*He turns Upstage Left.*) Brother Gabael of Rheges, I come from your kinsman, Tobit of Jerusalem, now of Nineveh! See, his seal bears witness. He asks for the return of the ten talents of silver he loaned you eight years ago when he was Purveyor to King Shalamanser . . .

There is a pause and a bag of money comes sliding across the floor out of the darkness and lands at his feet: he looks at it.

What, no interest?! . . .

A smaller bag of money comes sliding out of the dark.

Our thanks, Brother Gabael . . . (*He turns back Downstage.*) Oh, ease my spirit, quicken me to the glorious light which gutters now. Why am I subject to this shame? I heard the Lord say, 'Let things be done decently and in order.' But there's no decency here, no order here, only disorder the final enemy . . . Yet, yet, yet, since all things come from Him, there must be good, even in that disorder, for it contains the possibility of change. I had become petrified in my certainties, now plunged in doubt and disorder, I'm given the chance to change and grow. That's the reason for God's

unreasonableness. Veils lift . . . a blade of grass is a
miracle as great a work as the constellation of Orion, and a
babe's head as round as this whole, round world.
Eternity's bonny light gleams for me once more and other
sounds from behind the sky are heard again . . .

*A dawn light comes up slowly Upstage Left with the faint
music of fiddles and tambourines, which grows louder.*

The Lord's acts make angels doubt. But neither angels,
nor men, should be afraid of that. Minds and hearts are
not meant to be fixed, immovable. Only by changing,
living, growing, do we blossom and become one bright
rainbow arcing earth, sea and sky.

*A clash of cymbals and dim figures are seen Upstage Left,
dancing joyfully.*

Scene Seven

*Lights up on **Tobit**'s garden, Nineveh.*

Raphael *stands by the broken wall, Stage Right, as the
dancing company approaches. It is **Tobias**, **Sarah**, **Anna**,
Tobit and **Raguel** pulling a cart stacked high and covered
with brightly coloured silks. **Tobias** and **Sarah** are decked
with flowers and the others festooned with ribbons as they
sing a bridal song.*

All (*singing*) 'Bride and groom. / Come home soon. /
Doves, doves, keep us awake. / Give them a piece of
wedding cake. / Doves, doves, flutter above. / This young
couple are in love.'

Tobias   Master Azarias? How did you get to Nineveh
before us?

Raphael   I flew. Your ten talents, Master Tobit, plus
interest.

Anna *picks up the bags.*

Anna Plus interest? I'm surprised. Now we can tell your father you're not entirely useless.

Raphael I'm sure my Father will be pleased, if He doesn't know already.

Tobit We're grateful for your help, Master Azarias. Be sure to take your fee.

Tobias I'm glad we've no need to go debt collecting again, Father. It is a touch sordid.

Raguel This is a pleasant spot. Good sheep country.

Sarah Mother, let's break bread in the garden before we enter the house.

Anna Spread the silk, bring out the food and wine. (*They spread the cloth on the ground and put the food on it.*) I'm in a rare mood. (*She sings.*) 'Praise be the Lord, we're no longer frugal. / See, we've beneplach nockerl and noodel kugel. / Try every dish. / From this fruit kissel to the gefilte fish. / Here, for my sake. / Don't forget this Passover Passion Cake. And you might give a nod. / To my freshly baked mandelbrodt.'

Raphael *takes* **Tobias** *aside.*

Raphael Tobias, I've one more task to perform. (*He opens a small pouch and hands a piece of meat to* **Tobias**.) This fish's gall. Rub it on your father's eyes.

Tobias Why?

Raphael Why? Why? Why? And again 'why'?! Because it will restore his sight.

Tobias This fish's gall? I'll look a complete fool if it doesn't.

Raphael That shouldn't worry you over much. There *must* be something in you, Tobias, otherwise the Lord, perverse as He is, wouldn't've chosen you. The gall has curative powers like the liver.

Tobias I don't fry it, do I? Well, I'll try anything to help my father . . . (*He crosses back to the others.*) I've been told this might make you see again, Father.

Sarah What is it, Tobias?

Tobias Fish's gall.

He rubs **Tobit's** *eyes with the gall.*

Anna I heard of all kinds of nostrum – wormwood, hellebore, lavender, senna, rams' heads, wolves' hearts, corns from a horse's leg but fish's gall, never, ever. Am I right, Tobey?

Tobit Yes.

Anna There, you see!

Tobit Yes.

Tobias Yes, what?

Tobit I can see.

Anna You can see?

Sarah See, see?

Tobit Yes, the sun's there, the grass here and the air's all around and Sarah, my new found daughter stands before me, beautiful as a rose in Eden and Anna the light of my eyes is in my arms.

He grabs **Anna** *and dances around with her amid shouts and laughter.*

Anna It's my son! Tobias has the great gift, the healing touch.

Raguel Does it work on sheep?

Tobias I don't know.

Raguel They're always going blind. And what about ringworm, tapeworm and gangrene?

Sarah Blessed be the Lord God of Israel. He has made Tobit see Tobias again. Let's embrace for the day of happiness and joy!

About to embrace each other, there is an ominous drum roll as **Ahikar** *and* **Kanach** *in full armour enter Upstage Centre.*

Anna I knew it was too good to last! Do you do us down again, nephew?

Ahikar We come from the king.

Raguel Is there trouble 'twixt you and the king? If I'd've known that, I wouldn't've agreed to this union.

Sarah I would.

Tobit King Esarhaddon's hatred never sleeps.

Kanach It does now.

Anna Why?

Kanach He's dead.

Ahikar We're talking of the new king, King Ashurbanipul – the Good.

Kanach The Very Good. He's promoted me General of the Imperial Guards.

Ahikar And made me Chief Cupbearer to His Person.

Tobit What of our people?

Ahikar Those out are now in. Jews are being buried six feet under like the rest, and you are once more Purveyor to the Royal Household as you were in King Shalamanser's time.

Tobit Praise be the Lord whose light shines over all regions of the earth.

Anna He no longer hides his face from us.

Rows of giant sunflowers spring up from behind the wall.

Sarah And Jerusalem shall be built of sapphire and of emerald and all the world resounds with 'Alleluias'.

A **Chorus** *chants 'Alleluia! Blessed be the God of Israel', as they move towards the meal spread out on the ground.*

But **Raphael** *gestures and the* **Chorus** *is cut off and all except* **Tobit** *'freeze' in their positions.*

Raphael It's time for me to leave and tell you the truth at last. I've been living a lie. I'm Raphael, one of the seven angels of the Lord, who sent me down to heal you and rescue Sarah. Of course, you wouldn't've needed healing if He hadn't injured you in the first place. But that's His way.

Tobit You're an angel?

Raphael Stinkin' now but that's only outward show. Inside, I shine with the light of Truth.

Tobit If you're truly an angel, you must've met my father, Tobeil, in Heaven when he died ten years ago.

Raphael I remember him well. On his deathday he was ushered into the presence of God seated on His golden throne studded with precious stones. 'Lord,' he said, 'does all this wealth belong to you?' 'Who else?' replied God. 'And is it true,' continued your father, 'time means nothing to you?' 'Yes,' replied the Lord, 'a thousand years and a day are all the same to me.' 'Well then,' said your father, 'could you lend me a million drachmas?' 'Tomorrow,' replied the Almighty quick as a flash.

Tobit That sounds like my father.

Raphael I told him he was going to have a good rest in Heaven; we had no burying or selling there. 'Of course not,' he grumbled, 'it's not where business has gone.'

They laugh.

Tobit I didn't know angels laughed.

Raphael They don't as a rule. But I've acquired a taste for it. I've changed. Not taken up a mountain high, but brought low to wriggle and crawl and suddenly I'm beyond myself. Born deaf and blind, now I see and hear and laugh as much at your antics as you should mine . . . Listen, listen, do you know the first thing Eve did when Adam came home late one night? She counted his ribs . . . (*He laughs; there is a clap of thunder.*) Ah, I'm being called home. I must be levitating.

He crosses to the wall.

Tobit May your halo never grow less, Angel Raphael. Any last words? You carry within you the wisdom of Heaven.

Raphael Don't be afraid.

Tobit Afraid of what?

But **Raphael** *only shakes his head and shrugs. About to step into the wall, he pauses at the last moment.*

Raphael Only remember, in the beginning was the word and the word was – gevalt!

Laughing loudly, he steps into the wall and disappears.

As he does so, the others resume moving towards the food on the ground and the **Chorus** *finishes chanting 'Alleluia! Blessed be the God of Israel!'*

Kanach Your God of Israel sounds a good one. He tests you hard but rewards you handsome. He's not the sort who forgets a favour.

Anna He saw who suffered most in His name, and He's repaid us at last.

Tobit More than you know. He sent down the angel Raphael in disguise as Azarias to protect us.

Tobias Where is he?

Tobit Gone back. But he told me before he left.

Sarah Azarias an angel? That would account for the many wonders we've seen.

Anna I told you there was something odd about him. The eyes – he never looked you straight in the face.

Raguel Let's drink in praise of the Lord who sent down a full angel to watch over us.

As they all drink, **Ahikar** *takes* **Tobias** *aside.*

Ahikar Was Master Azarias truly an angel?

Tobias My father believes it. He's old and has seen hard times. That can turn the strongest mind round and about. So, if he's comforted by believing an angel served us, then I'll agree. But, in truth, Azarias was just a wandering raggedy-arsed, beggar-man with nits in his armpit. Take my word for it, no angel he.

Ahikar And the wonders?

Tobias Me. I've got a certain winning touch, no question. I'm pretty resourceful, in my way. But if it makes father happy, I'll agree it was an angel.

Ahikar Diplomatically put. You have the makings of a first-class courtier, my boy.

Raguel Ba-ba-ba-baaaa, if my sheep could see us now. They love happy endings.

Sarah (*singing*) 'The time of happiness is here. / Oh, how sweet, oh, how dear. / Now we sing and dance with reason. How good are the deeds of our God in their season.'

All (*singing*) 'Go in peace, rain. Come in peace, sun.'

Sarah (*singing*) 'The storms are over and gone. / Winter has been so hard, so long. / Now we see a bright new day. / And the things created in beauty and placed in our way.'

The tall sunflowers turn their faces Downstage and sing in close harmony with the others.

All (*singing*) 'Go in peace, rain. Come in peace, sun.'

Sarah (*singing*) 'Flowers give forth their scent. / And the birds are meant. / To tell us all at last. / Sorrows too are past.'

Birds appear on top of the wall and join in the singing as a rainbow appears.

All (*singing*) 'Go in peace, rain. Come in peace, sun. / Earth is crowned with new wheat. / Creatures drowse in noonday heat. / We embrace each living thing. / When we dance and sing. / Go in peace, rain. Come in peace, sun.'

Lights fade down to a spot on **Tobit**, *Stage Centre.*

Tobit   Yes, but . . . My father told me the story of a famous fiddler who played so sweetly that all those who heard him started dancing. One day, a deaf man who knew nothing about music passed by the fiddler and the dancers. He thought they were all madmen. Their actions seemed so senseless. I'm a deaf man now. It all seems senseless to me. I'll live to a rich, ripe old age in the bosom of my family, continuing generation to generation. All this will be written of in the 'Book of Tobit' or 'Tobias', whichever you prefer. They'll get it wrong, of course. Writers always do, but what of that? We'll be revered – happy legends of a bygone age. But I didn't worship the God of Zion to be so rewarded. It's too easy worshipping a God who rewards you. No glorious leap needed for that. But to worship a God who is unknown, unknowable, who gives no sign, who makes no concessions, who punishes the good and bad alike – ahh, yes. That's true faith, true believing. It needs a special kind of man. I was that special kind when God tested me harder than He'll test Job. For Job will be punished because when he was Pharoah's advisor he didn't speak the truth. He kept quiet and keeping quiet always makes you an accomplice. I spoke out against injustice in deeds not words. Yet, God made me suffer. There was a glory there. Now it's gone and like Sarah, I shrink.

He sighs loudly.

God's Voice Tobit, with that sigh, you have lost your chance of Heaven.

Tobit (*looking up*) Good. Now that reward has been taken away from me, I can begin to worship you again in earnest. But I'm disappointed, Lord. Before, my heart heard You clearly in Your unending silence.

God's Voice I can't seem to do anything right for you, Tobit. Sitting alone on ancient peaks, man has been a mystery to me since the Fall, though I brought him forth in My substance. None of you rise up shedding pride, power, arrogance till you reach that good end and become gods yourselves. That's how it was planned but you remain stubbornly earthbound.

Tobit Because we are made of earth, of clay.

God's Voice No, of life and light.

Tobit Then give us a bigger part of your splendour, so we can rise.

God's Voice You have it.

Tobit Where are you, Lord?

God's Voice Where I'm allowed to be. Which means few places. And they grow less. Take care or heaven will become a sheet of burnished copper.

Tobit Then save us from thoughts like mine. I sometimes think there is no Judgement, no Judge, no God – God forbid!

God's Voice Why does that worry you?

Tobit Because if there is no Judge, what purpose is there in the world?

God's Voice If the world has no purpose, what concern is it of yours, pray?

Tobit But if the world has no purpose, what use is faith?

God's Voice None probably, but why should it bother you if faith is useless?

Tobit But if faith is useless, then all life is meaningless.

God's Voice And that troubles you?

Tobit Yes.

God's Voice Since you're so troubled by meaninglessness, you must be an honest man, and honest men are allowed to harbour such thoughts.

Tobit You don't mind?

God's Voice Who am I to mind? You're not unique. On other stars an endless succession of troubled Tobits roll past. And when this earth is cold as death and all mankind long since dead, in other worlds men like you will still wonder and still bleed. 'Tisn't my job to clump up and down every moment of the day with my big feet and set you all shivering. Life is a gift given to be lived that's all. Reject it and then perhaps you'll see me truly angry. One thing is worth remembering. Heaven above is conditioned by you below. So if you're charitable, Heaven too is charitable, if you're joyful, Heaven rejoices, if you sing, Heaven is full of song.

Tobit Ah, well, in that case . . . (*Singing*.) 'Raise your right foot. Drag your left foot along. Hop once, hop twice and bellow out this song.'

God's Voice (*singing*) 'Raise your right foot. / Drag your left along. / Hop once, hop twice and bellow out this song.'

Tobit ⎫
God's Voice ⎬ (*singing*) 'Bimbom, bimbom, bimbom. Bimbom, bimbom, bom. Hop once, hop twice and bellow out this song.'

Lights full up as **Anna**, **Tobias** *and the others sing and dance too. They are joined by the unseen* **Chorus** *singing high above them.*

All (*singing*) 'Bimbom, bimbom, bimbom. / Bimbom, bimbom, bom. / Hop once, hop twice and bellow out this song.'

Lights fade down as Heaven and Earth sing together for a moment.

Revolutionary Witness

Revolutionary Witness was first broadcast by BBC TV in July 1989 with the following cast:

The Patriot	Simon Callow
The Butcher	Alfred Molina
The Preacher	Alan Rickman
The Amazon	Janet Suzman

Produced by Margaret Windham Heffernan
Directed by Jonathan Dent

The Patriot

Palloy *stands in front of a skeleton, balls and chains, and a set of manacles. All have price tags and are hanging on a wall below the words 'Live Free Or Die'.*

On either side of **Palloy** *are neat piles of stones of various shapes and sizes, each marked with a price in white chalk. Elegantly displayed amongst the stones are various expensive gift-cases containing medals, pieces of wood and model replicas of the Bastille. All are priced. The whole effect is of a superior window display.*

Palloy (*singing*) 'Patriot Palloy, Patriot Palloy, on the sacred altar of Liberty / Laid his heart and his genius for all to see. / His heart he gave to his country. / His genius to his immortality. / Patriot Palloy, Patriot Palloy.' That's me, Citizens. Patriot, Entrepreneur, Architect, Songwriter, Soldier, Philosopher, Revolutionary and all round good fellow – Patrius Franciscus Palloy, the Messiah of Liberty. My card . . . (*He flicks out a card.*) No name on it, no name needed. Only the image of the Bastille, a sword, scythe and tricolour. That's enough to tell you it's Patriot Palloy himself who welcomes you to the grand opening of Palloy's Emporium, 20, Rue des Fosses, St Bernard, Paris, the exclusive purveyor of authentic souvenirs of the Revolution.

Citizens, Brothers, Fellow Republicans, history is nothing but decoration. Here it's for sale. These real Bastille stones washed clean by the blood of the oppressed and crying out 'Buy me! Buy me!' are precious mementoes of the most glorious day in the history of the world, July 14th 1789 when we suddenly walked light with our feet barely touching the ground.

Why should the old religion have the monopoly of holy relics? What're Moses' bones compared to the bones of an unknown never-to-be-named prisoner, found hanging in

the deepest Bastille dungeon, dead white and stinking?
These are our holy things now, and more precious far,
than the nails from the True Cross – and more authentic.
They may not cure diseases of the flesh but watch 'em
work their wonders on diseases of the spirit, for they
banish bitterness and despair in an instant and give true
believers radiant hope that centuries of oppression can be
overcome. They are carriers of light, light not from above
but from ourselves.

I've elected my Apostles to transport two hundred and
forty six cases of Revolutionary relics throughout the
provinces. Each Apostle will give a speech in the various
provincial capitals before handing them over to agents
who will sell them on commission. The old Church has
been making money out of their faith for centuries, now
it's our turn. Human beings find it difficult to value
anything, even Liberty, unless they've paid for it. I think
you'll find the new religion less expensive than the old.
Just look at the prices.

I'm not ashamed to admit I'm here to spread the good
word – and make a profit too. I learnt that from my father,
Georges Palloy. Just before he died he ordered me to bury
him with his hand left sticking up out of his grave in case
somebody passed with something he could grab. He
could've been a great man but he lived the life of a
cockroach. We all did in the bad days. My mother wore
herself out lighting other people's candles. Poverty makes
beautiful women ugly. We suffocated under tons of bird
droppings, now we can soar.

Some say we're building a new aristocracy on the ruins of
the old. We are, but it isn't a permanent class of vermin
like the old. It's an aristocracy of trade which changes
daily like the waves of the sea. Trade is the new force in
the world. It displaces hereditary privilege and physical
strength, calling forth powers that were left to rot in the
former age.

You see how we've all become philosophers now? I know there's no rational basis for revolutionary optimism given our lifelong weaknesses and selfishness. Either mankind falls back into darkness or else the Revolution succeeds and creates something new. This Revolution of ours isn't a short moment in which one power overthrows another but a long moment in which power is dismantled to bring into existence a society in which all powers will be done away with because every individual has full power over themselves. These stones will help build that society and make it strong. And any one of you can be part of it for as little as ten francs.

I'm selling the Revolution to the world. These stones, bones and manacles give everyone a taste of it, as they sit in warm corners. The New Americas are already my best customers. General Washington ordered a large stone, Citizens Jefferson and Hamilton splinters from a Bastille beam. Flanders, Italy and Austria all want to buy. There's a demand from every country, except England. The English aren't interested in Liberty: never have been. They're the most servile collection of flunkies left at large in Europe. They tried Revolution once. Killed a King even and took their first steps to freedom. But the experience was too much for 'em. They soon flopped back on their knees and they'll never get up. That's why they're fighting us now out of the shame for their long cowardice. They can't win. (*Singing.*) 'Our enemies we shatter / Their forces we scatter. / Our glory complete. / The sight of a free people. / No retreat, no retreat.' My own composition. Words and music. Two sous a sheet. You can buy copies on your way out. There's a full selection on display in the other room.

It's a patriotic song from a patriot. In France we can be patriotic without wanting to vomit. France is the Revolution and if we're for the Revolution, we're for France. So why not buy yourself a song and better still a medal, Citizens, and show the world you're a patriot? These medals inscribed with the motto 'Liberty or Death' are made from the chains of the Bastille drawbridge, chains we have the courage to break. In the old days such medals could only be bought by the rich. Ordinary people like us had to die gloriously on some forgotten battlefield before we were given one. Now they're on sale to all at ten francs each, whilst stocks last. Who's to say in years to come, they'll be less valuable than the starry ornaments pinned on the pigeon chest of some Court toady?

One thing is certain, you can take your place at the 'Feast of Reason' or the 'Feast of the Supreme Being' wearing your medals with pride. And it is important, Citizens, we attend our Festivals and Feast days fully rigged.

When I came to stage the 'Feast of the Supreme Being' in my home section of Sceaux I knew how to do it right. We started early with the sun coming up over the rim, new day, new hope and the town crier calling each citizen to pray to the God of their choice in their own manner. All the houses were decorated with flowers and we came out into the streets and embraced each other, swearing our hatred of tyranny and love of friendship. Thousands of people parading through the town square dancing the 'ronde national' and singing the 'ça ira'. Thousands of people and no police. I armed the marshals with sheaves of wheat instead of clubs and bayonets. A free people have no need of force to restrain themselves.

It was all a brilliant success. But success evokes enemies, especially in these times. Just as the Republic has its foes I have mine and they are the same – the envious, the weak and the fearful!

They saw their chance with the Tuileries fire. Some of you look puzzled. You don't remember. I never tire of telling the story because it illustrates even someone, such as I, whose spotless patriotism is known countrywide, is still vulnerable.

The Tuileries caught fire and I organized the team to put out the blaze and restore any buildings left standing. For that I was accused by the Minister of the Interior, the infamous Citizen Rolland, of not paying my workers and removing certain unclaimed items from the Tuileries. Oh Liberty, forever smeared and foul-mouthed had a friendly hand to tighten round your throat!

My dear wife pointed out all the workers had indeed been paid by the money raised by selling the missing items. How else? These are hard times and we must improvize. But the Minister wouldn't listen. He had a mind of his own which was probably his greatest weakness. We all live on the razor-edge of luck, Citizens, and I was clapped in prison and the case taken to the National Assembly. My wife and I selected our youngest daughter Simone to defend me.

She was seventeen, wild as a fawn, sweet as maple syrup, as beautiful in the face as any angel could be. She stood in the front of the National Assembly in the pure white robes of Liberty crying 'Patriot Palloy is innocent! My dearest Papa is without reproach! Long live Liberty, Equality and Fraternity!' And then she sang the 'Marseillaise'. The whole Assembly joined in, crying and singing and that grease-spot of history, Citizen Rolland, was lucky to escape with nothing worse than a broken arm and pelvis.

That bright figure of a girl defending her father won all hearts to the truth. Of course it helped she was young and beautiful and the delegates were all Frenchmen. But images are more important than words. Simone clad in white reminded them of my innocence just as these stones and beams, soaked in martyrs' blood, will remind you and your children of the Revolution. Through the years memories will fade and even those of us who lived through it all will wonder if it happened. My mementoes will be permanent proof it did.

Even now when it's still so near, I sometimes wonder if it was all a glorious dream. But I look on these speaking stones and I know I'm there again, on that first day, July

14th '89. I touch them, and the current of history passes through my fingers. I tremble and live that glorious day again.

Some say I'm not on the official list of those who took the Bastille. *Ha!* They say there was a Paillot and a Pallet but no Palloy – *ha!* So much for *facts!* That's what's wrong with dust-dry historians, they're only concerned with facts. Because it isn't written down they'll say it didn't happen. It happened. Palloy was there. I'm still there. I'll always be there.

Bread had just risen to fourteen and a half sous and the morning sun shone clear in a new sky as thousands of us marched on the clapped-out barracks of the Invalides all cockade bright with drums, fifes, tin whistles, shouts and cries. That great river of humanity swept up over the parapet to come face to face with a great cannon primed ready to blow us all to pieces. But Governor Besenval didn't fire. He was frightened of damaging a house he owned nearby. Dust-dry historians won't understand that those are the hidden hinges of history.

We took the Invalides, captured thirty thousand muskets but no powder or shot. But our blood was primed and we roared 'To the Bastille! To the Bastille!' Tens of thousands of us were on the march, artisans, workers, joiners, builders, carpenters, dressmakers, locksmiths, nailsmiths, blacksmiths, the oldest was Citizen Crétaine aged seventy two and the youngest little Lavalee, all of eight. But our leaders weren't there. Danton and Desmouline arrived after it was all over. It's when leaders usually arrive. It's what makes them leaders.

I remember the watchmaker, Humbert, was the first to climb one of the Bastille towers and then Citizen Davanne and Denain managed to let down the drawbridge and so we flooded across. 'To the Bastille! To the Bastille!' Governor Launey opened one of the outer gates and let us into the great courtyard. When it was packed tight the honourable Governor opened fire on us with his troops.

Volley after volley cut us down. Suddenly there was blood and death all around but we didn't flee or turn tail. We preferred to be killed, realizing at last it's less hard than dying. That was the turning point. We stood our ground and died there. But I wonder if we would have if it had started to rain. We'd probably have gone off home, Bastille or no Bastille, and would never have seized the chance to live free. How many times has bad weather changed the world?

Anyway we stayed and fought. Courage grows by daring, fear by delay. We set fire to a Santerre brewery cart filled with straw so the smoke filled the courtyard and the troops couldn't see us. Then reinforcements arrived with guns and cannon and mortar, and we could now fight back. There was confusion and disorder in the smoke and the dying, the screams and the groans and cries, but there was also true glory. Because you see, every man there was his own leader, and he followed his own impulses. Most of us had never handled a gun in our lives yet soldiers on the ramparts swore they'd never been under such disciplined musket fire; they couldn't raise their head above the parapets. We were no longer a mob but a free people fighting for life and liberty.

Suddenly it was over. The Swiss Guards refused to go on and the Governor surrendered. As he was taken away screaming 'Kill me! Kill me!' he accidentally kicked Desnot the baker straight in the privates, *ooohh, ahh!* Old Desnot collapsed clutching himself and groaning 'I'm done'. And some hot-heads stabbed the Governor, shot him six times and cut off his head. Pity, you could say he lost his head by kicking Desnot in exactly the wrong part of his anatomy. Anywhere else he might've survived.

But I was too busy to worry about Governor Launey. People were already stripping the Bastille bare. Taking anything that was takeable, free of charge. Looting was rampant. I immediately got it organized. The National Assembly made it official. That's how I came to have the sole rights to dismantle the Bastille. I think I've done my duty there, Citizens, as this Emporium demonstrates.

But in truth I never saw my job as merely tearing down tyranny's walls but also of building Liberty's ramparts. My dream is to build a Monument to the Glory of Liberty on that site. Naturally I've designed it all myself. There'll be houses, shops, gardens, covered walks, fountains, long straight streets. The Street of Victory, the Street of Legality, the Streets of Equality, Abundance and Renewal. Dream streets, dream gardens and fountains, but we'll make them real. There'll come days that will be short and we'll sleep long but now, it's up and doing! Buy my goods, Citizens, buy 'em and then join me in building the future. It won't be a Utopia of cloudless skies but it will be better. Instead of Bastille darkness we'll have Palloy light. Up and doing, Citizens! Up and doing! Can't you feel the joy of living a life that sings! *Aeeeee*. (*Singing and dancing.*) 'Liberty is dear to us, Happiness is near to us / Joyfully appear to us / It's all clear to us / Up and doing Citizens. / Up and doing! . . .' Don't forget, Citizens, individually signed copies of this speech can be obtained on your way out, priced three sous. History is yours for less than a glass of Spanish wine . . . (*Singing.*) 'Liberty is dear to us / Happiness is near to us / Up and doing, Citizens / Up and doing!'

The Butcher

The National Assembly is in session. **Robert Sauveur**
*stands on a small rostrum in a bloodstained leather apron, a
meat cleaver and knife stuck in his belt. His sleeves are rolled
up and his arms are flecked with blood. A huge tricolour flag
covers the wall behind him.*

The chatter of the unseen audience dies away.

Sauveur I can't read, I can't write and I'm no speaker.
I'm a journeyman butcher – Citizen Robert Sauveur and
I've come straight from the butcheries of Sceaux to this
Assembly, not powdered, scented or booted but with the
blood of a slaughtered ox still warm on me. I'm here to
present a petition for the Ponceau Section. I don't know
why I was given this honour. I have no qualifications
except if need be, I know how to plough a field, mend a
roof and a pair of shoes and I've always earned a living
with my hands. But I'm not educated or clever. Yet I'm
here on behalf of all sorts and kinds of peoples, water-
carriers, caterers, porters, locksmiths, labourers, glaziers,
gauze-makers and the rest.

But before I can speak for them I must present my
credentials. It's important to know what I am. I come
from a family of ten or twelve. I'm not sure how many.
Most of them died before I was six, of the sweating
sickness and starvation. Put all human suffering on one
side of the scale and poverty on the other and poverty I
think would be heavier. With poverty you are in fear of
everyday things like old age, sickness, an increase in the
price of bread, a rainstorm that stops you from working,
the birth of another child. It's hard to keep a fingerhold
on life when the smallest change can make you fall even
lower than you are.

All us children had different mothers and I don't
remember mine. My father was a butcher and like most,

worked, drank and whored quickly through his life. He
was spared old age. Strength was all he had. With that
gone, he'd've been a bundle of rags, bent double begging
outside a church. Instead he died, damned, cursing me.
They were deadish times, long winters, short springs.

I started killing when I was thirteen. One livre a day for a
twelve hour day, five a.m. to nine p.m. in the summer. I
often worked by moonlight, though you don't look up at
the moon much when you're busy. I can't say how high
the moon is from us but it's higher than Notre Dame so it
meant nothing to me. We did most of the butchering in
the streets round Saint-Jacques, Montrouge and Gentilly.
There was always a heavy stink of blood about those
places. Blood, rot and death. We'd chant: 'Now's the time
Henri, begin the knocking. Spread them out upon the
floor. Get them ready for the hammers. Tie them down
and let them roar. Keep them still and then knock 'em.
On their marks let them drop. Keep their heads and feet
from piling. Do not let the killing stop.' Between the
slaughterings the men would drink and huge whores
would sit on small stools showing themselves off to
shrieks of laughter.

There were shrieks of another kind from the steers as we
started to slaughter them. They'd be thrown to the
ground, horns tied with rope to a post and we'd smash
their skulls with a mallet. A knife would slit open their
throats and bellies and the blood poured out in torrents
which women caught and made into soup with a few
herbs. Then we'd pull out the entrails and hack the
carcass to pieces and hang it up for sale, still steaming.

Sometimes butchers'd be too drunk to kill the steers with
the first blow and they'd escape smashing down anything
in their path. But the butchers rushing after them were
more dangerous. It was money on the hoof to us and we'd
club down anyone who'd get in our way. I killed two men
by accident like that and three in brawls but they hardly
counted. It happened when we were drunk. We were

always drunk and we thought if things ever change for the better we'd be even drunker. A friend said to me, 'When the Revolution comes everything will be wonderful, the Seine will be brandy.' I said, 'Why not the Mediterranean? If you're going to believe in something, believe in something big!' I was right there, but most of the time I was stealing food from somebody else's plate and dogs would bark at me in the streets. I lived like the beasts I killed. No difference except I was full of rage and hate and I didn't know why.

I joined the army and fought in some battles, mostly in mist and fog. I don't know where or even who the enemy was. No fame or glory there. I left after a year. It was too tame after Paris. I went back, took up my old trade and old ways.

We didn't understand anything. A man I knew who dealt in horses and leather said he'd been married a year and still hadn't had any children. 'To tell you the truth it's a family sickness. My father didn't have any children either,' he said. 'What about you,' I said, 'where were you from?' 'Oh,' he said, 'I was from his first wife.'

I used to live with a number of women in cheap lodging houses which we'd leave nights without paying the rent, stripping the room and taking the doors and floorboards with us. The first woman I won in a card game and lost the same way. One girl with red hair – I don't even know her name – I bought for a bottle of wine and a salad. She stayed with me for six months and then went missing. Nothing lasts always. She was hooked out of the Seine a week later. I found her one morning, hung up by her feet along the riverbank with the others, wet and dripping – rows of them.

I got another woman that afternoon – that was easy – we slept together dead drunk in the butcheries with a cold carcass for a pillow. But it wasn't the same. I remembered the one in the river and an extraordinary thing happened, I began thinking of her. I'd avoided thinking all my life –

what good was it? Yet here I was doing it. Leave my mind alone! Leave it alone! But it was no good. I thought why does she hang there like meat and not others who should be hanging? But the terrible thing about thinking is that it just doesn't stop, does it? It goes on and on. One thought is too many, a thousand aren't enough. Why are there things and not other things? Why is it this way and not that way? I'm a simple man with a small head. I wasn't used to it. It was like having a fever in my mind. I could hardly think, I was doing so much thinking.

Up to then my ears had been as deaf as adders but now I heard voices for the first time, from every hall and open space in the city. There were prophets every day before our eyes, walking up and down the street and they gave dust, and those that were less than dust, a tongue. They began to get hold of me in some kind of way when they spoke of freedom and the Rights of Man. From them I heard that in the beginning there was no rich, no poor, no bondage or servitude, no one person above another. That all came afterwards by violence and cruelty. I learnt that all men and women stood for freedom and only the privileged were ashamed of it and that virtue was an active force, manly and virile. The old world was falling, and through a crack in a closed door I saw a light like two suns and I made discoveries of the truth that had lain hidden in darkness.

Then even the flies used to bite but workers put up with all their miseries, not because they're too stupid to do anything about it but because they're too tired. Day and night, winter and summer, heat and cold, sun and moon, work is woven into the fabric of their lives. That and nothing else. After working the slaughtering street fourteen hours, all we wanted to do was sleep and drink. But now suddenly we had energy to spare. It was everywhere leaping like a living flame from man to man, woman to woman. It consumed us, the zeal and the fire, and we had the strength to turn the world around. Liberty isn't a scrap of paper called legal rights. It isn't being free of something. It's liberty to *do* something, *be* something!

I was there when the National Assembly proposed that there should be less pride, less holding back one with another. No more bowing and scraping and taking off hats. We were no longer to be called Monsieur and Madam but Citizen and Citizeness. Now I was to be a citizen where before I'd been a beast without dignity.

All things changed, even the dress we wore. Before, when they got it too easy and spent it too soft, there was lace and ruffles and silk ribbons and the women wore their hair piled 'hedgehog' style high above their heads, decorated with fruit-bowls and tiny zoos with animals and a small pond. Now our hair is worn natural and we have plain trousers, open shirts, jackets and boots. Small things compared with Europe at war, France in turmoil but the everyday exists alongside the heroic and sometimes is more important to ordinary people like me.

Dress changed, and I changed with it because I felt I could make a difference. I didn't want to be left behind. I had to rise out of the mire in which I lived and make myself worthy of the Revolution which remade me.

I married the widow Fabre. She already had two children and I fathered two more. I have a beautiful etching of us all together made by Citizen Dufois . . . (*He fumbles in his pocket, then stops.*) No, perhaps another time. Yes, another time . . . We live in a large house in the Ponceau Section on the third floor at 130 livres a year for two rooms. If all goes well and my children work perhaps one day we'll move down to the lower floors where the rents are anything up to 700 livres a year, but that's a dream and dreams are never certain.

I'm still a journeyman butcher, slaughtering in the same street my father lived and died. But I don't whore or gamble and only drink a little wine because it is healthy. I do my civic duty now nights, and attend the political meetings of the 'Society of the Friends of Liberty and Humanity' over in the Graville Section. I paid the entry fee of one livre and four sous and now I help pass resolutions and listen to speeches and debates I don't truly understand though I try, I try. But the handbell opening the meeting, the Declaration of the Rights of Man stuck on one wall, the president's chair, the plaster busts of Brutus and William Tell and the hall full of great orators have become part of my life.

And when one of my friends like Jacques the shoemaker reads out by the light of the lamp we bought together, the decrees of the National Assembly and we discuss them and argue and then finish the session by singing Revolutionary songs, I know I belong. This is the way it should be. People like us should never need politicians, we must do the governing ourselves.

To make a man moral you have to make the world he lives in moral too. And that can only happen when there is liberty and justice for all. As for me I'm no cleverer but I'm trying to be honest as this world goes. I know honesty in a man often means he will deceive himself first. I hope that's not the way it is with me. If you can't be good, act it because if you act something you are it. Now I think of my life as a trust to be used for a good purpose and accounted for when it's over, which is why I suppose they call me Robert the Virtuous Butcher. I know it makes my friends smile, especially those that knew me before. I smile too, but I'm not ashamed of the name. Robert the Virtuous Butcher – it has a ring to it.

I'm sure that's why I've been chosen to present this petition for those revolutionaries who are asking for justice from the Revolution. The only question in any crisis is 'What can I do?' When the time came they asked it and acted. Everything else is a waste of energy. The only question, for a sensible man is 'What is to be done?'

You remember, Citizens, the 6th August '93, the Prussian army was breaking through at Verdun? It was only a matter of time before France was defeated and the Revolution crushed. All our best hopes gone down in blood. The Saint-Antoine Section warned this Assembly that the treacherous king must be deposed or suspended by the 9th or the people would take action. On the night of the 9th we did, and the forty-eight Sections from the Roule to the Gobelins formed a commune and the toscin sounded the alarm and the people of Paris marched to the Tuileries and the king's palace. There were thousands of us there that night making sure the Revolution wouldn't die.

We had no leaders. We didn't need leaders and their orders. We'd all heard too many orders – a lifetime of orders. We knew what we had to do without 'em. They called us a mob because of it. But we were no mob, just plain men and women taking destiny in our own hands for a moment. I know, I was one of them and I was surrounded by friends.

When we reached the Tuileries some of the men from Marseilles wanted to talk to the Swiss Guard guarding the palace. They thought they might be able to get them to lay down their arms. We warned them it was dangerous. In the Reveillon riots of '89 the authorities killed hundreds, the rioters not a soul. In the fall of the Bastille we lost one hundred and fifty good men and women, the defendants only seven. In the fight in the Champs de Mars only two loyalists were killed whilst fifty of our people were slaughtered. Violence is authority's weapon and they're not afraid to use it.

But the men from Marseilles wouldn't listen. The Swiss let them in and then opened fire. Three hundred of us died that night in the courtyard, dying like oxen on the hoof. I know, I see beasts die every day. We killed the Swiss later for their treachery and stupidity too, because the king had already gone and they were defending an empty building, bricks and mortar.

Soon after, the king was finally turned out for good and we defeated the Prussian army. The Revolution had been saved that August night. We'd won a great victory. But nothing comes free. Winners suffer as well as losers.

I'm here to speak for the winners. You won't find their names in any book or roll of honour. I'm talking of the men who died or were wounded taking the Tuileries and are now rejected. Men like Pierre Dumont, aged thirty-two, a gauze-maker, who was killed that night and leaves a widow who had received no pension; Antoine Lobjois, aged thirty-nine, a glazier, killed leaving a widow and five children without a pension; Louis de Roy, aged twenty-one, killed at the first gate leaving a mother, wife and two children and denied a pension; Pierre Homelle, aged forty-nine, journeyman watchmaker, lost an eye attacking the courtyard and refused compensation; Henri Bute, aged forty-one, labourer wounded in the leg and refused compensation; Louis Chauvet, aged twenty-four, water-carrier, a hernia scaling the walls and refused compensation.

The maimed will probably die from their wounds one way or another and their families with them. Crippled they can't work and if they can't work they starve. These are men I know. But there are others treated in the same way. I have a list here. (*He pulls out a paper.*) Good men and women, our own people, but officials, civil servants, doctors, remnants of the old gang, have refused to sign certificates of compensation for them in order to save the nation a little money. Civil servants are born with souls like that. But we revolutionaries are not. I know France is at war and every sou must be made to count. But this is a matter of common justice which is why we fought in the first place.

My wife came up to the window in our bedroom this morning and opened it so the air could come in. I could see grass and sky and sunlight everywhere. It seemed an old but beautiful world. And I thought we must cleanse it of all evil, violence and oppression so we and future generations may enjoy it to the full. It'll be a long journey to that new world. We must pick up those who fall on the way and carry them with us.

Citizens, the Revolution can act stupidly because it is human, but never meanly or ignobly, it is too generous and noble a cause. Honest men like Henri Bute and Pierre Homelle are being treated like liars. They aren't liars. But if you don't believe them, believe me. They are honest and brave and they fought and died for us. The Revolution made me and I don't lie. So let us honour our debts, pay what is due to them and move on. We've a whole new world still to make.

The Preacher

*Late afternoon. A priest, **Jacques Roux**, in a cassock with
a dagger stuck in his belt, speaks from a battered pulpit.
Behind him, a broken stained-glass window of an angel with
a flaming sword. His dog, Georges, lies curled up on the floor
beside him, a red, white and blue rosette attached to its
collar.*

God created rich people first and then showed them the
world they would own and when they came to a field with
thousands of headless bodies with torsos and hands like
iron, God told them the headless bodies were destined to
be poor workers. The rich cried out 'But these heroes
with their iron muscles will crush us.' 'Don't be
frightened,' answered God. 'I shall place very small heads
and brains on their bodies, so until they develop them
you've nothing to fear.'

Who're still the oppressors? – the rich. Who're still the
oppressed? – the poor. Your slavery is their liberty, your
poverty their prosperity. Priests say the poor must be
content with their poverty and they'll have heaven
hereafter. Idiots, cretinous rag-pickers! My dog, Georges,
has more sense. You can have heaven here and hereafter
too! You suffer, bleed, die without learning anything.
Don't you know whilst you're gazing up at heaven your
pockets're being picked clean, eyes plucked out and
you're robbed of your birthright, blind to what is done to
you?

Christ's priests seized mankind in its cradle and broke the
bad news saying 'You shapeless stench. You can never be
anything but filth. Your only chance of winning a pardon
for being so filthy is if you bow low in perfect humility in
the face of all the afflictions, sorrows, and injustices
heaped on you. You're poor and you stay poor, that is
how it is meant to be. Life is a bitter ordeal. Don't speak

out. Just try to save your worthless soul. You won't be able to, but you will give us less trouble by trying. And when the time comes for you to die croaking, the darkness will be as hard to bear as the daylight ever was.' Oh the Church knows its business. It offers fear and punishment, not happiness, certainly not liberty, only servitude, forever and forever.

Religion is a liar and a cheat yet still you hunger for it. That's why you've sent for me, Jacques Roux, Mad Jacques, Red Roux, Preacher of the Poor, sower of sedition, subverter of all laws, a priest who saw the light of reason and now proclaims fellowship with all who live in dark dens and desolate places. It's fitting I should preach, perhaps, my last sermon in a ruined church in the parish of St Nicholas, summers end.

I go before the tribunal tomorrow, charged with revolutionary excess. Now, I am, it seems, too revolutionary for the Revolution. And so it begins. When power reigned in one man, King Louis, all sorts complained of oppression and the nobility, middle and monied men called on the poor to help. Together we lopped off that top branch of tyranny but the tree still stands and spreads. New branches hid the sun of freedom for the poor, the revolutionary tribunal is one such. I don't recognize its authority to judge me. Only the poor of St Nicholas can do that. I come here to lay the rags and tatters of my life before my peers. Habits are hard to break, Citizens. I come to confess me. Hear my confession.

Do not forgive me Father, for I have not sinned. My own father had twelve children and as I was the cleverest he rid himself of me by sending me to school at the Angoulême Seminary. At fifteen I was ordained a priest when I knew even less about God than I do now. There was a priest on every dunghill, the scummier they were the better they sprouted. But I stayed on and became Professor of Philosophy travelling roads leading from nowhere to nothing, pronouncing without practising, aspiring without attaining, teaching students to bear with fortitude the misfortunes of others. Like religion, philosophy solves the problems of the past and the future, never the present.

In '79 the Angoulême students rioted over the agony they saw around them and killed a cook by accident. As a suspect teacher with ideas I was arrested and imprisoned, though I had nothing to do with the incident. A month or so later I was released. No trial, no inquiry, authority had decreed it and I had no say in the matter whether I was to be free or in chains. This is how fires are kindled.

Afterwards I spent four years in the Chair of Experimental Medicine at Angoulême. No more philosophy, endlessly cogitating the universe. But medicine proved equally useless. Physicians know even less than philosophers and priests gangreened together with no cures for the pain of living. They lie, they all lie! Isn't that so Georges? You tell them, I've grown hoarse in the telling.

In '89 I was given this poor parish of St Nicholas and I was born into the real world of starvation and disease and I saw the horror and the hope too. For the Revolution burst over us, smashed the clamps that held us down and swept us up, up with its transforming power. We opened the book we'd never read and on the first page was the word 'Liberty'.

Listen, listen, the Revolution was born in violence. Revolutions must be violent, it's the only way to end the greater violence that keeps the majority of mankind in servitude. Do you think those with privileges would give them up without a fight because you have a charming smile and the best arguments?

Adjuro! Adjuro! I renounced my alliance to Rome and gave it to France. I became a constitutional priest, put off the mitred robes of privilege and put on the white robes of

Liberty. No longer a mumbo-jumbo man – into the sewer with the whole breed of moralizing bloodsuckers.

I still practice as priest and physician when called on but not sustained by unjust tithes and church taxes wrenched out of other men's labours. I had to earn an honest living as a pamphleteer and municipal official.

I live with a good woman, widow Petit, born Elizabeth Hubert, once laundress to the rich, now my helpmate, soulmate, who sells my pamphlets two sous a copy. We adopted a son, Emile. A sweet, sweet boy . . . No more of them. Not for your ears or yours or yours. My only fear, Citizens, is not of death but of a life without them. Georges knows. We love them don't we, Georges, eh?

I was elected a member of the Commune and spoke for the poor. I told Robespierre, Saint-Just, Brissot, Herbert and the rest that they could never be the Revolution. There were only men and not to be trusted with power. Anyone with authority becomes an oppressor, a parasitic coat of filth on the hide of the common people. Between those who command and those who obey there is only hate. Does it follow that I reject all authority? No, but I always keep my hat on in its presence. In the matter of bread I consult a baker, in the matter of boots, a bootmaker, a house, a builder. For special knowledge I apply to a specialist. But I don't allow the baker, bootmaker or builder to impose their authority over me. I listen to them with the respect they merit – if any – but I keep the right to judge, criticize and censure. Why should we treat politicians of whatever stripe, royal or revolutionary, any different? I listened to King Louis, Mirabeau, La Fayette the same way I listened to the baker and the bootmaker. Don't be fooled by those who set themselves above you. Always look at the bill they are presenting – you have to pay it.

And criticize me too. People thought Citizen Marat and I were enemies because we were ever attacking each other. He called me an extremist, this from a man who declared three hundred thousand heads weren't enough. But we were never enemies, just revolutionaries, doing our duty. Yet neither of us were popular with the legislators. Not my purpose to be popular. I'm here to sting!

To stop me stinging the Assembly hired me to write the report of the king's execution. We didn't do that well. But you'll not squeeze one tear from my eyes over the fate of a royal fool and his followers who talked of honour and died without it. To the boneyard with the whole crew. (*Singing.*) 'The rich we'll gobble up / Tra lee, tra low, tra lie / With truffles in the rump / And oysters on each eye.'

I love the harp. That's how men and women should die – to the sound of harps – they are so precious. King Louis died to the sound of drums. The Republic had already substituted the Rights of Man for the Divine Right of Kings and Louis as a symbol was already dead. Louis the man was of little importance so why did they make such a fuss about killing him?

We drove through the streets lined with citizens. Give the public what they want and they'll turn out no matter what. Louis mounted the scaffold in silence. They had three executioners waiting – three! And eighteen drummers! What extravagances just to kill one man.

The knife fell and Louis' head fell with it. The crowd shouted 'Long live the Republic' and then I saw Santerre and the other Revolutionary officials dipping their handkerchiefs in the king's blood. More reactionary relics, splinters from the crumbling cross. What titanic imbecility! Mealy-mouthed lickspittlers to the bottom of their whorish souls.

I wrote it all up in my report but I was the only one who seemed disgusted by the whole spectacle. Invading armies were about to overwhelm Paris, there was civil strife in the Vendee, rebellions in Lyons and Bordeaux and good men and women were dying everywhere defending the Revolution even as the traitorous Louis was dying on the scaffold. But the good and the true had no carriages, no eighteen drummers or three executioners, a Prussian sword in the belly, an English bullet in the chest and falling face down in the mud was their end. That's how ordinary people die, meanly, without harps or even drums to play them out. But Louis, that useless toe-rag of a man, goes in style, his anemic blood gathered up as something precious.

A month later, remember, I led the attack on the Paris food merchants. I'm proud of that action, though those in power condemn me for it, so I know it must've been right. We ask only for food, a home, a little ease, no more crying in the streets 'Bread, bread for God's sake!' But in that bad winter there was nothing but war, famine, and miseries piled on misery. We were at war so we accepted such hardship if they were equally shared. But they weren't. We were dying because of filthy bourgeois graft and greed, the slimy rapacious money-mad exploiters were hording food to raise the price on the open market. Our legislators wrung their hands, threatened in a whisper and did nothing, so women and children starved before our eyes.

Then we flat-bellies marched, smashed stalls, broke into shops and warehouses and found the bread and meat and other foodstuffs they'd hidden in abundance. They asked why we took it and we told them it was because we needed it. Citizen Marat said we should kill every merchant in sight. We made do with a few score strung up in front of their own shops to encourage the others. And it did. Next morning the food markets were filled again with fruit, vegetables, bread and meat. Like Jesus we had performed a miracle of the loaves and fishes.

We must appropriate land and money from the rich who have it in excess and give it to those who need it and live in want. My petitions were thrown out as being too inflammatory but the only way to defend and save the Revolution is by pushing it as far as it will go and then further – and that's never far enough for me.

Then Citizen Marat died, steel through the heart, painless when he had such a painful life. I miss him. No one left to trust. That's why I agreed to become editor of his paper when his staff asked me to keep the bright flame burning. So when those excremental conformists, Robespierre and the Jacobin gang, banned women from political power we took up the cause. They wanted to keep liberty for themselves alone. I wrote that those refugees from the leper house of reaction should be belled and booted head first into the nearest sewer.

In return they persuaded Marat's widow, Catherine, to denounce me to the revolutionary tribunal for besmirching her husband's memory. Poor sweet, Catherine. Grief takes many forms. She wanted to protect her husband's fame and thought I was taking it from him in some way. I shun fame. It always costs too much . . . (*The sun begins to set behind the stained-glass window as a harp is heard playing gently.*)

Late last night I went walking through the streets of Paris with Georges. Just the two of us, Georges padding beside me sniffing every post and doorway and me smoking my pipe – oh there's nothing better – making love perhaps, or making a revolution but with a revolution you have to be right. It was a clear night and empty streets but as we passed St Nicholas Church something strange happened. I was walking but suddenly I couldn't hear my own footsteps, not one, silence . . . I was a dead man walking.

No more of that. (*The harp music stops.*) Tomorrow before the tribunal of mumblers I shall make no attempt to defend myself. That doesn't mean I'll stay silent. Never that. I'll do what I was born to do – attack. If the verdict of that bunch of rotting fish-heads goes against me I die like friend Marat, though struck down by a better hand – my own. (*Gestures to his dagger.*) The Ancients said the good man must walk alone to a right death. You win by losing.

It's been a rich confession after all friends, deserving of some penance, at least five Hail Marys and twenty six Amens. After all I've preached revolution and sedition, slaughtered a king and others, lived in sin and will probably end even deeper in it by killing myself. In the eyes of the Church it is a hundred percent record of failure. But on Judgement Day I expect to stand before my God justified. I do not condemn myself and shall not be condemned.

And so amen. (*A glorious sunset behind the stained-glass window begins to illuminate the angel with a sword.*) If it's to be the last amen I go gladly. My wife and son will weep, I know and Georges here will howl a little won't you boy? Friends will pause and shake their heads and move on. For they have the difficult part. Living well is so much harder than dying well. They'll remain whilst Mad Jacques Roux will become at worst an obscure footnote in history. I haven't done anything bad enough to be included in the main text.

I've tried to help create a people who are sceptical, rational, critical, not easily fooled or impressed. In a word a free people – ungovernable! It's a dream of course but I've been lucky to have lived through times that made the dream seem possible, when for a moment, we stopped being me and mine, you and yours, us and them, and saw ourselves instead as equals in our common humanity. We are of that generation that so transformed the world that future days and nights can never be the same. We poor, clumsy, men and women turned the world upside down, inside out, round and about. (*The angel with the sword glows in the fiery sunset.*)

One last word from my last sermon. The Revolution isn't complete, hardly begun. Defend it. Don't sit back – act! Without action no life, without life no perfection, without perfection no eternal peace and freedom. For God is an active power, so we do His work in fighting the great battles, light against darkness, love against selfishness, revolution against reaction, life against death. Come on Georges, it's time for our walk!

Quick fade out as he whistles for Georges.

The Amazon

Dressed in a worn nightgown **Théroigne de Méricourt**
*sits on a wooden chair in the centre of a bare cell in
Salpêtrière Asylum, 1817. There is a solitary window
behind her.*

Liberty, Equality, Fraternity, Liberty, Equality,
Fraternity, Liberty, Equality, Fraternity, my brain
splinters, the words die, rot, or go mad like me, curtains
drawn across my face. I ask them for water and a piano-
forte and they send me stale bread and second-hand
cherries. My head rubbed tight between two cloths, not
saying what I think, not thinking what I say and no truth
unless it's wrapped in so many lies it can't be found. So
I'm sitting in a room where everything stops and the God
of Panic grips my throat. What do you expect? You're
Théroigne de Méricourt, the one and only and you were
devoured bleeding, boneless, with the rest. Revolutions
aren't made with rose water and lace fans: d'Herbois
deported, Condorcot poisoned, Marat stabbed,
Robespierre, Danton and Saint-Just guillotined, Pétions
eaten by wild dogs, and I'm not feeling too good myself
locked and buried in a madhouse, the smell of fish and
dead eyes behind every door. Someone came here years
ago to ask me to write my memoirs and I said I hadn't the
time, I was too busy being mad. (*Singing.*) 'I, like a ship in
storms was tossed / I had to put into land. / Once in port
the vessel's lost / My cargo was contraband.' So I end in
the jaws that swallowed Jonah, Salpêtrière Asylum 1817,
where I hang my heart upon a willow, weeping. Hold.
HOLD. I'm sitting but my spirit is still upright, at right-
angles to my body, I'm still Théroigne de Méricourt,
dead to the world but never weeping.

The wonder is that such things are and others things are
not. Some women are born lucky, like blown glass they

shatter easy. But I come from peasant stock and the bright stars were dark at my birth so I survive, torn apart by ghosts with webbed feet. (*She takes out a small hand mirror and looks at herself though there is no glass in the frame.*) Look at me now, livid, blotched, and mildew all over. Buried in the dark for twenty years, sick dawns and pale heartbeats. It's natural. Of course there's no mirror in the frame but I don't need one. I know how I look. (*She puts the mirror away.*) Just as I know I was lithe and lovely once. I had Helen's hair and men marvelled at my beauty.

What a sham identity is. Born Anne-Josèphe Terwage on the river Ourthe, forty miles from Liège. Repeat and repeat the story else you'll lose all sense of who you are and what you've done and your life will drift away down and you'll become mad. So repeat and repeat though there are only flickering ghosts who listen out there.

The bird in my head tells me first love is the hardest to forget. (*Singing.*) 'Youth's a season made for joys. / Love is then our duty' . . . He was young and handsome as a crow but what was his name? He was English. I know because we eloped to that green and pleasant land where the whole system only works to sustain privilege and protect status. My lover wanted to give me everything – his money and his name but his family objected and he obeyed like a true Englishman. They always come to heel in the end, born to obey, men with bad teeth, always making washing movements with their hands. They dared not even pity themselves above a whisper.

There are things money can't buy, but in those days, those weren't the things I was interested in, I was dancing a minuet to the music of men and women being tortured. I had other lovers, some lasted at least until breakfast. I think I even had the Prince of Wales, soft in my bed. I did, I did, stale underwear over fat, white, flesh.

Then the Marquis Armand de Parsan fell madly in love with me. There's a word, 'madly'. I was much younger

than Armand but I felt old age creeping up on me every
night. I sold myself for excitement, travel, two hundred
thousand livres with fifty thousand placed out on interest
and two bankers, Monsieur Perregaun of Paris and Mr
Hammersley of Ranson, Morland and Hammersley of 57
Pall Mall, London. A good bargain I thought then and if
I'd've continued in the way of business I would've ended
my days in a chateau in Salpêtrière, not a mouldering
asylum, eating wet straw. BUT I always went down my
own road, let Hell blaze as it pleases. Doors opened and I
preferred new errors to old certainties. The quest not the
goal. What counts is the action however desperate, what
counts is what is missing and never found.

I was combusted, burnt to a cinder, first for money and
men, then for music, sovereignty was in me when I sang.
(*Singing the aria 'A Change How Deceiving' from Gluck's*
Orphee and Euridice.) 'A change how deceiving. / Repose
I am leaving. / Once more to be grieving. / At life and its
pain.'

I had the voice then, gone now, like Armand, who said
singing wasn't what he was paying for, oh no. I wanted to
be the best so I hired Tenducci, the best teacher in
Europe. Friend of Mozart who wrote a piece for him, that
should've warned me. Mozart had no morals and
Tenducci had no plug-tail – castratos have it hard. He
reminded me of that other limp lubcock Robespierre, who
also had legs like spaghetti and nothing much between
them.

I like men but I don't esteem them. I've been betrayed
too often. After Tenducci I was lost and I went in search
of myself on the road to Paris and Damascus '89 where I
opened my inner eye – the one here in the middle of my
forehead. I wasn't blinded like Paul. I saw for the first
time the world decoded.

Bang, crash, ahhh, history moved, and burst into flame,
the Bastille fell and joy was in the air, abounding and
abounding, illuminated by visions, ideas, insurrections,

and I was consumed by revolutionary fever, swept up,
ebony into gold, suddenly a precipice, white water,
rainbows and kingfishers rejoicing and rejoicing. Oh what
a storm the light was then, when our evenings touched
our mornings!

In ordinary times we don't think the world can be any
different from the way it is or ever will be world without
end. But at certain moments in our lives when it falls to
pieces – a sudden death, an illness, a parting – then the
sky splits and the earth heaves up its milk. That's how it
was in those early days, balloons rose in us on honeycomb
breezes. It was the beginning of the Revolution – before
the idea of revolution existed. We uttered one word and
altered the rhythm of existence. When I looked up
'Revolution' in the dictionary it was only a word derived
from the verb 'to revolve'. We gave it new meaning, we
gave everything new meaning.

Men made the Bastille fall but we women made the march
on Versailles. Hunger was the reason, bloated bellies
floating down every alley. I spoke and continued to speak,
my inner flood never failed. 'Where is the bread? – at
Versailles!' 'Where are the tyrants? – at Versailles!' Three
thousand women marched that day pistols and pikes,
cudgels and halbards. I rode a black horse in a riding
habit of red silk, red plume on my helmet, pistol and
cutlass in my waistband singing and dancing on the way
to Versailles. WRONG. The fluid passes. Is it smoke I
see or has the mist come at last? Gaps spread and
memories cannot furnish the truth. There was no singing
and dancing that day. It was raining and the women were
too weak. I didn't lead the march, I was already at
Versailles when they arrived. But it's a good story and I
believe it.

The king's militia were waiting for us, muskets primed. I
told the women there was one way to make sure they
didn't fire, so we met them with roses in our hair, arms
bare, skirts up, smiling. When men are hard, they are soft.

I'd learnt something from my former life, to carry with me.

The king made promises he didn't keep and Marie-Antoinette saw me and ran away so fast her hair came down and she scattered a shower of white powder as she ran. Later the Châtelet Law Court issued a warrant for my arrest, and I fled to Marcourt where I was kidnapped by royalists and carried off to the Kufestein fortress in Austria. Exciting, isn't it? I'm excited just remembering. All emotions time-tamed to a whisker now, but my spray-blown days were so full then, empty now, sucked dry and the world full of daggers.

The Emperor Leopold charged me with attempting to kill his idiot sister Marie-Antoinette. I was in prison, locked and bolted, longing for liberty. Now locked and bolted, longing for death. Why don't you come? 'I am Death, say goodbye to the white world. I will cut through to your bones.' Oh yes! Oh yes!

The royalist press rejoiced at my capture. Newspapers are vehicles for the suppression of every generous impulse, night-carts for tyranny and oppression. The editor Surleau wrote of my immorality on the sound journalist principle of first besmirching your victim's morals before you destroy them. 'Théroigne is the most terrible of females. Whose inexhaustible paps / Like street taps / Offer drinks for sale / To every passing male.'

The Emperor sent for me to come to Vienna where they all bow from the hips. Despite the trappings of power, Leopold was the kind of man you'd like to have with you when you wanted to be alone. With a little effort he could have been anonymous. But if a slug becomes a king you bow, so I dressed carefully, white robes, hair loose, no powder.

He attacked me for my democratic fanaticism. I said 'You condemn the Republic, that is your duty. I condemn the monarchy, that is mine. I have only one hope, that the principles of the Rights of Man should spread throughout the world. I have a crystal conscience. I didn't try to kill your sister. If I had I would've succeeded.'

The Emperor did not answer. He was a man of few words. He only knew a few and was in truth more interested in my involvement with the Prince of Wales. History after all is only gossip. I told him the Prince took all night to do what some men do all night. He agreed it was his brother-in-law Louis' trouble too. I was freed soon after but I insisted Leopold pay my expenses home. It was only right. I never wanted to go to Vienna did I? Did I?

'Long live Théroigne! Long live Théroigne!' How Paris loved me when I returned. At the Jacobin Club they gave speeches in my honour – the Fair Martyr of France, the First Amazon of Liberty. Oh the energies of '92, the golden glass made manifest, no more walls, the world so big it lost all horizons. Now I stand alone looking out to sea in an old skin that doesn't fit but then life bubbled, boiled and laughed. I was always moving, never tired, reading, writing, making speeches, seeing that there were two fights – for the Rights of Man but for the Rights of Woman too. I thought since men and women are alone they must help each other and so break out of their solitude. Surely it was the moment for woman to emerge from the shameful insignificance in which the IGNORANCE, PRIDE and INJUSTICE of men had enslaved them? No longer beggars at the feast. I asked the Cordelier Assembly to give women a vote – a woman's word flying in the face of history. So they considered and considered and considered and declared, though a woman had a soul and intelligence which could be used for the good of the state, they couldn't give her a vote. And these, friends, remember, were the best of times, the best of men. Light the black candles of fear, I felt madness was upon me even then, the air full of grey flakes falling softly on my soul.

But I fought in the light of reason. Since all the political clubs were for men only I formed the Saint Antoine District Club for Women. Women spent three evenings a week in reading and discussion and social work and young girls were taught trades in our workshops. But husbands and lovers didn't approve. The children were not being looked after, clothes not mended, dinners not cooked, wives not in their places. Our leaders naturally agreed, Robespierre who always wore a corset tightly laced, disliked women, d'Herbois despised them, Danton used them, only poor Marat had sympathy for us and he was killed by a woman, dimlaped down to dust.

At least, when I killed a man it was the right one. I saw the once mighty newspaper editor, 'paps like taps' Surleau, seized by the crowd in the courtyard of the Feuillants. I didn't strangle him with my bare hands. WRONG. It was more like suicide. We made him eat his own editorials. Choked on his own venom, killed between his weak jaws, gasping loudly, spitting blood from his ears. No regrets there, with one journalist less the world had to be a cleaner, safer, place.

In the days before the Revolution we couldn't walk through Paris without covering our shoes with blood from the heads and hearts split on pikes for stealing bread. And what of after? When that belly-scratching, short-arsed Corporal slaughtered millions? No one kept count: numbers sanctify. Where violence rules only violence wins. It's why I organized the Women Battalions. We had to learn to drill and fight, we had so much to defend – the abolition of slavery, full freedom for Protestants and Jews. And so much more to win. But ringed by fire we had first to destroy the enemies outside. Robespierre preferred the internal ones, closer at hand and they were endless.

Remember, remember that June day with the sun shining outside the National Assembly and hordes of Robespierre's harpies attacking anyone they thought was against their leader. That's me! That's me! 'Citizens, Robespierre is strangling Liberty. Are you free men and women? Will you let this happen?' The female hordes knocked me down and flogged me senseless when I called Robespierre a hairless, half-dead, cod-fish. Ah the women, first they kill poor Marat, then they try to kill me.

They said I was broken by the beating. WRONG. Only heartbroken because I couldn't hear the mermaid singing and was losing words like Liberty, Equality and most precious of all, Fraternity.

Fraternity . . . Oh what a beautiful word that was. When Deputy Lamourette told the Assembly that all our troubles came from one source – our own hatreds and what was needed was more brotherly love, more Fraternity, deputies who had been at each other's throats were on their feet hugging each other, all quarrels forgotten. But it didn't last of course, and men once more talked like men have talked for centuries and so missed each other. I saw demons and the rings of Saturn melt and despair hung from me in clusters.

My brother Joseph had me committed to save me from Robespierre's wrath. I was walled up by the law and by language, walled up alive, a relic of the Revolution, mad in a world where the sane have learned to sneer at words like 'brotherly love' – I know I can see through walls. You live by other standards now and I'm left beached from other times, when we grasped wholes not halves, from all things one thing, from one thing all, and we didn't see ourselves as separate, the leaders and the led.

Like all things the Revolution was doomed to falsehood and decay. We tried to burn away distinctions and bring about a true Fraternity. Failed, fragile as angel-dust in sunlight. The dream dying and the dreamer left bleeding. But we don't lower ourselves by our failures, only by our excuses. We saw one great truth – everything is changeable. All you have to do is stand on your haunches, no longer old trees with knots. (*A bright sunbeam shines through the windows behind her as she suddenly stands up in it, her face transformed in the warm light.*) The Revolution was a radiant city with shining towers and palaces and orchards full of fruit – we saw it! Dust like Carthage now. But twenty years mad in my desert cell, racked and riven by the black, the vision never faded. Twenty years, hard, for a glimpse of Paradise. And I'd pay it again, oh yes, yes, yes, oh yes, yes, yes! The Revolution's crushed, trampled underfoot and the good seed lies buried with me. But one day green shoots will thrust to the sun and stretched before us will be fields and fields of immortal wheat and in those fields those lost words will once more stir my blood and pierce me to the heart, Liberty, Equality, Fraternity! Liberty, Equality, Fraternity! Liberty, Equality, Fraternity! . . .

Lights slowly fade out.